Passing the Baton

How To Build a Four Generation Legacy

Robert Strand

Book Three in *The Power of the Blessing* Series

Mobile, Alabama

Passing the Baton
by Robert J. Strand
Copyright ©2013 Robert J. Strand

All rights reserved. This book is protected under the copyright laws of the United States of America. This book may not be copied or reprinted for commercial gain or profit.

Unless otherwise identified, Scripture is taken from *THE HOLY BIBLE: New International Version* ©1978 by the New York International Bible Society, used by permission of Zondervan Bible Publishers.

Scripture marked KJV is taken from the King James Version of the Bible.

ISBN 978-1-58169-476-5
For Worldwide Distribution
Printed in the U.S.A.

Evergreen Press
P.O. Box 191540 • Mobile, AL 36619
800-367-8203

Contents

1. What Is a Legacy? 1
2. Principles for Legacy Building 8
3. The First Generation: 17
   Abraham and Sarah; Ishmael and Isaac
4. The Second Generation: 26
   Isaac and Rebekah; Jacob and Esau
5. The Third Generation: 34
   Jacob, Leah, Rachel, Bilhah, & Zilpah
6. The Fourth Generation: 46
   The Children of Jacob
7. The Generational Covenant Blessing 51
8. Your Family Legacy 63
9. How Do We Build Our Legacy? 79
10. Passing the Family Blessing to the Next Generation 91
11. Live To Be One Hundred and Twenty 110
12. Questions To Ask Yourself 129

Appendix A Suggested Blessings To Use 143

Appendix B Building Your Plan 149

Appendix C Planning for Heritage, Legacy, & Dynasty 150

Appendix D Resources for Healthy Living 151

Dedicated to all...

Who are living in the blessing and...

Who now will pass it forward to the next generations and...

Who will be planning to impart before we depart this world and...

Who will be impacting this world with righteousness and blessing!

Introduction

Since I wrote the first book on the blessing, entitled *The B Word*, this subject has just kept on growing through my life experiences. As a family, we have adopted many of these concepts from the Torah (first five books of the Bible) and from the Jewish people. After writing and speaking about the first concept—the power and purpose of the family blessing—I wrote a second book about the power of the blessing to break generational or family curses. Continued study and speaking about the biblical concepts just naturally evolved in the book you have in your hands—how you and I can build a four generation legacy.

All of us are leaving a legacy behind—some of it is bad, some is indifferent, and some is good. How will you be remembered? How can you leave something intentionally for the next generations that will be valued and passed on to another generation? My interest was piqued. After more study and research, I found that it is possible to intentionally build a four generation legacy.

Now there are three books in this blessing series. I feel that the circle of information is more complete—from the blessing, to the power of the blessing, to the legacy of the blessing. The older I become, the more importance the blessing and all of its ramifications have become.

My prayer and hope is that you too will be challenged to intentionally build your own four generation legacy! What follows are some simple suggestions and insights in how you can do it.

May the Lord bless you and keep you
and the Lord be gracious unto you
as you begin this exciting journey of

**BUILDING YOUR OWN
FOUR GENERATION
LEGACY!**

—Robert J. Strand
Springfield, Missouri 2013

ONE

What Is a Legacy?

Let's begin by sharing two true stories...well, in reality, three very interesting stories about building a legacy.

Story Number One

A number of years ago, Al Capone virtually owned and controlled Chicago. Capone was not famous for anything positive or heroic. He was notorious for enmeshing the Windy City in everything from bootlegged booze to gambling to prostitution and using murder and mayhem to enforce and protect his illegal activities.

Capone had a sharp lawyer nicknamed "Easy Eddie." He was the Capone's lawyer for a very good reason. Eddie was good, in fact, very good. Eddie's skill at legal maneuvering kept Big Al out of jail for a long time, in fact, too long.

To show his appreciation, Capone rewarded Eddie and paid him very well for his services. Not only was the money big, Eddie received many special dividends as well. For an example, he and his family occupied a fenced-in mansion with live-in help, round the clock protection, and all of the conveniences and luxuries of that day. The estate was so large it filled an entire Chicago city block.

Eddie and his family lived the high life of the Chicago mob and gave little consideration for the atrocities that went on around them. However, Eddie did have a soft spot. He loved his only young son dearly. Eddie made sure this son had nice clothes, cars, money, and the best education. Nothing was withheld from him, and price was no object.

In a paradox of living, Eddie even attempted to teach the young man right from wrong. Eddie made it plain that he wanted his son to become a better man than he was.

Yet, with all his wealth, influence and connections, there were two things he could not give his son: a good family name or the power of a good example!

One day, after much soul-searching, he came to a very difficult decision. Easy Eddie wanted to rectify the many wrongs he had done. He decided he would go to the authorities and tell the truth about Al "Scarface" Capone. He would attempt to clean up his tarnished name and reputation. He would do this so he could offer his son some semblance of truth and integrity. In order to do this, he knew he would, in court, have to testify against the Mob. He also knew this would cost him his life and that his days would be numbered. So he testified in court with enough evidence to put Capone away as well as many of the Mob members.

In less than a year, Easy Eddie's life ended in a blaze of

gunfire on a lonely Chicago street. But, in his own eyes, with the sacrifice of his life, he believed he had given to his son the greatest gift he had to offer at the greatest price he could pay.

When the police arrived at the death scene to begin their investigation, they removed from his pockets a rosary, a crucifix, a religious medallion, and a poem he had clipped from a magazine. The poem read:

> The clock of life is wound but once,
> and no man has the power to tell just when the hands will stop,
> at late or early hour.
> Now is the only time you own.
> Live, love, toil with a will.
> Place no faith in time.
> For the clock may soon be still.
> *(Author is unknown)*

Story Number Two

Some years later we come to World War II, a war that produced many heroes. We will focus on one such man, Lieutenant Commander Butch O'Hare. He was a fighter pilot assigned to the aircraft carrier *Lexington* stationed in the South Pacific doing battle with the Japanese military machine.

One time, he and his entire squadron were sent out on a mission. After he was airborne, he looked at his fuel gauge and realized that someone in the flight crew had neglected to top off his fuel tank. He would not have enough fuel to complete his mission and return back to the Lexington!

He radioed the flight leader who commanded him to return to the carrier. Reluctantly, he dropped out of the formation and headed back to the fleet. As he was returning, he saw something that turned his blood cold! A squadron of Japanese aircraft was flying its way toward the American fleet.

When the American fighter planes left on their mission, the carrier and the rest of the fleet were all but defenseless. There was another complication—his radio was unable to send a warning about the approaching danger! There was only one thing to do. Somehow he must divert the incoming Japanese attackers from reaching the carrier.

He quickly put aside all thought of his personal safety as he dove into the formation of Japanese planes. With his wing-mounted .50 caliber machine guns blazing, he attacked one surprised enemy plane after another. Butch wove in and out of the broken formation and fired at as many planes as possible until all of his supply of ammunition was spent.

This didn't slow him down—he continued the assault. He dove at the planes, attempting to clip a wing or tail in hopes of damaging as many enemy planes as possible, which would cause them to crash or make them unable to continue to fly.

Finally, the exasperated Japanese squadron took off in

What Is a Legacy?

another direction to return to their base or carrier. Deeply relieved, Butch O'Hare (don't get ahead of me at this point and the connection you have probably made about his name and Chicago's O'Hare Field), and his tattered fighter limped back to the carrier.

Upon arrival, he reported in and related the events surrounding his return. The film from the gun-camera mounted on his plane told the story. It showed the extent of Butch's daring attempt to protect his fleet. He had, in fact, destroyed five enemy aircraft. This took place on February 20, 1942 and for that action Butch became the Navy's first "Ace" of WWII and the first Naval Aviator to be awarded the Medal of Honor!

One year later Butch was killed in aerial combat at the age of twenty-nine. His home town would not allow the memory of this WWII hero to fade away and today, O'Hare Airport in Chicago is named in tribute to the courage and heroism of this man.

The next time you find yourself at O'Hare International, give some thought to visiting Butch's memorial displaying his statue and his Medal of Honor. You will find it located between terminals one and two on the main concourse.

Okay, what do these two stories have to do with each other and the concepts of building a lasting legacy?

Butch O'Hare was Easy Eddies only son! So how cool is that? Now you know the rest of the story as Paul Harvey used to say!

Passing the Baton

A legacy is anything left to the next generation. Let's turn that a bit and think of a legacy as a way in which we can outlive our natural lives! There is something innate in all of us that desires to leave something meaningful for the next generation that will live on after we have departed this life.

The vast majority of us are just common folk—not famous, not stars, not international figures—just us. We eat out at McDonalds, we yell from the bleachers at the ball games of our kids, we change dirty diapers, we wear sweats and tees showing who our favorite ball teams are, live in humble houses that constantly need repairs, and pay our bills. We don't have live-in servants, we don't have chauffeurs, we don't have elaborate or 24/7 security, we worry about our health—we're just common folk. Abraham Lincoln said, "God must love common folks because He sure made a lot of them." That's us.

And we wonder is it possible that God can use us to make the world a better place? Can we raise our families to be world changers? Can we build a long-lasting legacy? God can use us and we can make a difference! He can use just regular folks like us! And He still does!

So how do we do this? Where do we start? Is there a pattern that we can follow? Are there instructions tucked away somewhere? What are the secrets to building a four generation legacy? Thankfully there are no big secrets and we have a blue print left for us to follow in building a legacy so that we can outlive our lives. The answers are in

What Is a Legacy?

"The Book" and the people who have already done this have left how-to-do-it instructions already written for us. The Book is the Word of God and the people who have already done it are the Israelites, God's chosen people.

There is no evidence that God only chose extraordinarily talented people, high class people, genius types or the very wealthy! The one thing the people He used had going for them was their willingness to take a step out of their comfortable boxes to follow Him! Therefore, congratulations, God can change your world through you because He uses people just like you and me! So it's time to "Just do it!" as Nike proclaims! And if you listen well...you will hear Jesus gently say, "Follow Me!"

TAKE AWAY TRUTH: In spite of how horrible or difficult the past may be...it's still possible to pass on a legacy and something positive to the next generation!

TWO

Principles for Legacy Building

Are you thinking, "Where is the third story promised in the opening paragraph in chapter one?" No, I didn't forget. Here is the story:

Jonathan Edwards was married in 1727. He was one of the American colonies' most respected preachers. He is best remembered for his dramatic sermon titled, "Sinners in the Hands of an Angry God." This sermon sparked a revival in the New England area. His preaching was so powerful that people grabbed the backs of the pews to keep from falling into the abyss that Edwards described.

What is not so well known is that he was a loving, caring father of eleven children. His practice was to spend an hour a day, every day that he was at home, with his kids. He would sit in a special chair with the little ones on his lap and the older ones on the floor around his feet. He would talk with them, read to them, answer their questions and more. But the most important action was that he took time to pray and speak a special blessing over each child, every day!

Principles for Legacy Building

A writer, A. E. Winship, in 1900 set out to prove how effective were the prayers and blessings in this family, so Winship managed to track down fourteen hundred (1,400) descendants of Jonathan Edwards. In the book he published, this single marriage produced an absolutely amazing, even awesome lineage. Here is what his legacy included:

- 285 college graduates! (Remember this happened in the 18th & 19th centuries.)
- 300 preachers!
- 13 college presidents!
- 65 college professors!
- 100 lawyers and the dean of a law school!
- 30 judges—local, state and federal!
- 56 physicians and the head of a medical school!
- 80 holders of public office!
- 3 United States senators!
- 1 Vice President of the United States!
- 1 Comptroller of the United States Treasury!

(A. E. Winship, Jukes-Edwards: A study in Education and Heredity, New York: Hard Press, 2006)

There is more to this story—the flipside. Look it up and continue this account with a comparable study of a man and family named "Juke" (who were contemporaries of Jonathan Edwards) in which you can see the devastation of the descendants of a very evil man. There are shocking contrasts.

Do the spiritual seeds planted into the hearts and souls of children pay off? Yes! You too can plant such seeds of love, joy, faith, meekness, grace, mercy, positive character, the promises of God, the Word of God, and how to live productively in today's 21st century! It is possible that your family can plant a family tree that will become a long lasting legacy of godliness for at least the next four generations and more!

Our study will take us into the lives of the first four generations of the nation of Israel, beginning with Abraham. We'll get back to these generations following this chapter. First, let's continue with the theme of how to outlive your own life, God's way!

Have you ever taken a close look at the Jewish culture and particularly the Jewish family and seen how to build a sustainable, long lasting four generational family? Without a doubt it's easy to see Jewish successes in today's world. How do you account for their exceptionalism? I understand that not all Jews are successful, take for example a Jewish family that returns to Israel from some foreign land in a poverty stricken state. But take into consideration the Jewish people as a whole, especially those who have found their family success in the covenant of family building and wealth building as given to them by God in the Torah (the first five books of the Bible). How do you make sure the family continues generation after generation? There is help and there are positive easy to understand answers!

Let's begin by taking a look at some mind boggling facts about Israel which many of us may not know. Here are some of their accomplishments that can be measured in facts and figures.

Did You Know?

- Israel is only 1/6 of 1% of the landmass of the Middle East.

- Israel has only 2% of the population of the Middle East.

- Israel's Gross Domestic Product (GDP) is larger than that of Egypt, Syria, Lebanon & Jordan combined.

- Israel has the highest ratio of university degrees and more scientific papers presented per capita in the world.

- Israel has the highest number of scientists, technicians, engineers, physicians and PhDs per capita in the world...by a large margin.

- Israel is the only country in the Middle East where Christians, Muslims and Jews are all free to vote and where women enjoy full political rights.

- Israel has more museums, orchestras, books, books translated and books read per capita than any other nation in the world.

- Israel has the largest number of NASDAQ listed companies outside of the U.S. and Canada.

- Israel developed cell phone and voice mail technology.

- Israel developed the Pentium 4 and Centrino processors and produces them.

- Israel was the first Middle East country to launch a satellite, the "Ofek 1."

- Israel has the world's most impenetrable airline security and the largest fleet of F-16 fighter aircraft outside of the U.S.

    (The above statistics are provided by John Anthony of "Bridges for Peace" and Joel Rosenberg)

Also you may be interested to know that Israel's dairy cows are the most productive and contented cows in the world. They average 25,432 pounds of milk per cow per year, compared to just 18,747 pounds from American cows; 17,085 from Canadian cows; 13,778 from European Union cows; 10,207 from Australian cows; and 6,600 from Chinese cows! Even in farming they seem to be ahead of the rest of the world, according to John Anthony.

But along with their success in life, it's not been easy for them. It seems that the rest of the world, except for the United States and Canada, are doing all they can to wipe out Israel and the Jewish people.

> Of the United Nations Security Council resolutions passed before 1990, 97 were directed against Israel! Of the 690 UN General Assembly resolutions voted on after 1990, 429 were directed against Israel! (John Anthony)

And still they flourish and succeed all out of proportion to their size!

Let's make another comparison. Since the Nobel Prize has been awarded, the Muslims and the Israelites both claim Abraham as their progenitors. The Jews have followed the teachings of the Torah, while the Muslims have been hi-jacked by the prophet Mohammed, the moon god

Principles for Legacy Building

Allah, the Koran, and their teachings. Look at the following comparison:

Since the Nobel Peace Prize has come into existence in Sweden, between 1901 and 2012, the Muslim/Arabic/Islamic world who number some 1,200,000,000 which is about 20% of the world's population, collectively have been awarded eight (8) Nobel prizes. (One of these was given to Yasser Arafat for peace? Go figure.) Another was given to Albert Camus who was born to French parents but was raised as a Muslim in North Africa.

The Jews number approximately 14,000,000 of which about half live in Israel and the others are scattered world wide, account for about .2% of the world's population, which is a about equal to the population of Nepal or Morocco. They have won or been awarded 10 in literature; 8 in peace; 22 in chemistry; 13 in economics; 45 in medicine; 31 in physics, plus others for a total 158 Nobel prizes. (Perry Stone claims this total is really 176.) Think of it in this way...less than .2% of this world's population have been awarded more than 22% of the 750 Nobel Prizes. I remind you again that both groups of people claim Abraham as their father, but they have chosen different life philosophies—one based on the Torah (first five books of the Bible) and the other based on the Koran. (These statistics have been taken from Perry Stone, and Joel C. Rosenberg from his book, *Epicenter*).

When my wife, Donna, and I were traveling through Poland, our travel guide stated that "Of all the European countries, Poland has been awarded more Nobel Prizes than any other nation because of the Jews who lived and worked in Poland." (The Jews who are descendants from Medieval Jewish communities and live mostly in Northern Europe are called Ashkenazi Jews. Incidentally, when tested in a study, their I.Q.s were an average of 15 to 20 points higher than the populations in which they lived!) These are powerful testimonials to the intellect and life style of the Jewish people who have lived by the Judeo-Christian ethic.

How about another comparison? According to the *CIA WORLD FACT BOOK, 2012 EDITION,* the gross domestic product (GDP) of the Middle East Countries, the immediate neighbors surrounding Israel are:

Country	Population	GDP
Lebanon	4.1 million	$63.7 billion
Jordan	6.5 million	$38.7 billion
Syria	22.5 million	$107.6 billion
Egypt	83.7 million	$537.8 billion
Israel	7.6 million	$247.9 billion

With three times the population of Israel, Syria has less than half of Israel's GDP. With eleven times the population of Israel, Egypt has only a little more than two times the GDP. The only conclusion that I can come up with that stands the test of time is that God's blessing is still evident on the life and legacy of the Jewish people!

Principles for Legacy Building

The Jewish Legacy!

Mark Twain wrote the following article which is taken from an issue of *Harper's Magazine* in 1899:

> If the statistics are right...the Jews constitute but one percent (1%) of the human race. It suggests a nebulous dim puff of star dust lost in the blaze of the Milky Way. Properly the Jew ought hardly to be heard of, but he is heard of, has always been heard of. He is as prominent on the planet as any other people and his commercial importance is extravagantly out of proportion to the smallness of his bulk. His contributions to the world's list of great names in literature, science, art, music, finance, medicine, and abstract learning are also way out of proportion to the weakness of his numbers.
>
> He has made a marvelous fight in the world in all ages and has done it with his hands tied behind him. The Egyptian, the Babylonian, and the Persian rose, filled the planet with sound and splendor, then faded and passed away; the Greek and Roman followed, made a vast noise, and they are gone. The Jew saw them all, beat them all, and is now what he always was, exhibiting no decadence, no infirmities of age, no weakening of his parts, no slowing of his energies, no dulling of his alert and aggressive mind. All things are mortal but the Jew; all other forces pass, but he remains. What is the secret of his immortality?

What is their secret? We could pile up a whole lot more to make the argument that they have been and still are an exceptional people group with extraordinary accomplishments in their life and the outstanding contributions they are making in today's world. It all began with Abraham and a new beginning called "The Blessing," and it became a covenant sealed in blood for a nation—a people of destiny. This was then renewed and has been sealed and re-affirmed with the blood covenant of Jesus Christ for all of us. Therefore we need to understand that the Jew and we as the Church, all come from the same family tree and are intertwined until all the promises of the covenant of blessing are for us, Gentiles, even in today's twenty-first century! It's as old as Abraham and as new as today!

TAKE AWAY TRUTH: There is a plausible reason why the Jewish people and the nation of Israel are so exceptional. It can be traced back to Abraham and God's covenant of blessing which also is our covenant of blessing in today's world!

THREE

The First Generation: Abraham and Sarah, Ishmael and Isaac

Ur was a cosmopolitan metropolis of 2200 B.C. and was celebrated throughout the civilized world as a center of commerce, culture, and religion. This city was a marvel of architecture and design with paved streets and a subterranean sewage system. The middle and upper classes lived in large, multi-storied homes with hot and cold running water. All enjoyed the prosperity and luxuries made possible by Ur's international trade and commerce. It was located on the Persian Gulf at the mouth of the mighty Tigris-Euphrates rivers and was populated primarily by Sumerians who are regarded as pioneers of human systems and civilizations. They constructed the first great temples and towers, and created the first system of writing so as to record their rich legacy for posterity. This was a very sophisticated urban setting and a very attractive place to live!

Religion dominated the activities of this city. The chief of Ur's many deities was the moon god known to the Sumerians as "Nannar" and to the Semites as "Sin." Joshua later referred to this god when he said that the fathers of Israel worshiped other gods beyond the river Euphrates (Joshua 24:2-8). This worship was ostentatious and impressive as its cult and rituals were grossly perverted, pandering to the sensual and materialistic side of humanity. Abram and his father, Terah, must have been caught up in this system, which served and placated the pagan god "Sin" and all his pantheon of other gods.

So who would want to leave such a wonderful metropolis and become a nomad and live in tents in the desert? This city was conquered by the Guti, and for a hundred years (2180– 2080 B.C.) these barbarians imposed their inferior culture on the sensitive people of Ur, causing many of their citizens to flee rather than endure the indignities of the Guti occupation. It's thought that Terah was among those who chafed under this new regime and decided to move. Abram was born only 14 years after the Guti conquest in 2166. Terah took the initiative to leave, a fact explained only by his personal dissatisfaction in Ur because there is no evidence that he ever came to a faith in Abram's God.

This destination is significant—he went to Haran, a Semitic city populated by the Amorites, the second major center of moon-god worship after Ur. At last Terah died and Abram at 75 was now on his own. *(The above historical information was provided by Eugene H. Merrill, FUNDAMENTAL JOURNAL, April 1986.)*

Whatever did happen to Abram, one of Ur's leading

citizens, to enable him to become the man who was entrusted by God with a new covenant and a new life and a relationship with a monotheistic God? Obviously he forsook the worship of the moon goddess for the next 100 years of marvelous, awesome things that would happen to him. The importance of Abraham's life must be understood. The relationship between God and mankind changed drastically with the life of Abraham.

Before Abraham, as shown in Genesis 1-11, God had dealt in an all encompassing, general way with nations, peoples, and civilizations. Beginning in Genesis 12, God focused on one man and his descendants. Look at it this way...heaven had used a floodlight approach, which now was replaced with heaven's spotlight. Abraham became the focus!

The best overview of his life is given in the following:

> *By faith Abraham, when called to go to a place he would later receive as his inheritance, obeyed and went, even though he did not know where he was going. By faith he made his home in the promised land like a stranger in a foreign country; he lived in tents, as did Isaac and Jacob, who were heirs with him of the same promise. For he was looking forward to the city with foundations, whose architect and builder was God* (Hebrews 11:8-10).

His parents named him "Abram," which means "honored father"; and at age 99, God renamed him "Abraham," meaning "the founder of nations." That is quite a difference! And his wife was also renamed by God.

It's important that we take a close look at his wife, Sarah. We need to understand that her part in the blessing was enormous! God revealed Himself to Sarah more than once; He honored her as well as her husband. Sarah was changed forever because of the blessing. Her name was changed; her lifestyle was changed. You will note when looking at her life that she was a vital part of this family team and structure. She was a take-charge kind of a partner. She expressed her opinions. She demanded changes. She was not a silent partner that simply stood by as life happened. Do not overlook the importance of the partnership that is to be shared equally between husband and wife in living with and passing on the blessing!

She no longer was named "Sara," meaning "contentious"; her name was changed to "Sarah," meaning "princess." She was the princess of the Abrahamic covenant of blessing! This divine timing was perfect. In less than a year, the "Founder of Nations" and the barren "Princess" would conceive and bear a child together—Isaac! Wonder of all wonders!

But God was not finished with this man and his wife and their first descendant. There was a test for Abraham to pass. This test took place on Mount Moriah, just outside the ancient city of Jebus (Jerusalem). We all know the story of how God had asked Abraham to offer up his son, but a substitute sacrifice was provided at the last moment. God chose this event to reveal a new name for Himself, "Jehovah-Jireh," the "Lord will provide!" He did provide for Abraham, Sarah, and Isaac plus reveal something about

Himself in the process! So He will do the same with us in the 21st century!

It's important that we understand the historical background so that we can understand most or at least many of the implications of The Blessing and how we can also build a lasting four generation legacy. This story has all kinds of specific truth and concepts to understand while you lay a foundation for your family to build upon for the generations that will follow.

We'll not take the time to go into further detail about Abraham and Sarah here, but I will give you an outline that will give you a place to start. I strongly suggest that you make an effort to study an overview of their lives.

- Abraham's conversion (Acts 7:2) and his calling (Genesis 12:1; Joshua 24:3; Acts 7:3).

- The establishment of the blessing and covenant in his life and future of his descendants and how to bless the world (Genesis 12:2-3).

- His caution, his relationship with his father and other family members (Genesis 11:31-32).

- Coming into the land of promise, Canaan, and the building of his first altar and the act of worship (Genesis 12:4-9).

- Look at his carnality, his humanity, his flesh, his weakness, his ability to tell a half kind of a lie to protect himself and the cover-up (Genesis 12:10-20).

- Note his courage, his willingness to fight, his love and concern for other family members as well as preparedness to do battle (Genesis 14:1-16).

- The way in which he celebrated his victory, his generosity, he established the principle of giving and tithing (Genesis 14:17-20).

- He was an astute judge of others and made sure that all glory would be directed to God and not to any one else and took personal responsibility (Genesis 14:21-24).

- His compromise and the consequences of listening to others, taking another wife while loosing sight of the promise of God to him (Genesis 16:1-15).

- Don't overlook his obedience to God as the rite and covenant of circumcision was established personally and for members of his household (Genesis 17:1-2, 10-27).

- God makes the name change from that of honored father to now the founder of nations, Abraham (Genesis 17:3-9).

- The care and compassion for family and others is evident in his pleading with God to possibly spare Sodom and Gomorrah (Genesis 18:1-33).

- Another compromise but also included is how God looked at Abraham and protected him and his family (Genesis 20:1-18).

- Abraham faces the ultimate test of his obedience to God,

this could also be called the "Calvary" experience (Genesis 22:1-24).

- The last acts of his life, a new wife, his last will and testament, the passing of the blessing to the next generation and his home-going (Genesis 25:1-11).

- The focus of his life, looking for and preparing for the ultimate, the city of God, built by God and inhabited by God (Hebrews 11:8-10).

What an awesome founder (Abraham) and princess (Sarah) of a new life, the way to live, the way to follow God, what an example! Take some time to look over the above history and note the life principles...which can also serve each of us as to directives for our living and lifestyle!

As we come to the last chapter in the life of Abraham, a question comes to mind: Did the blessing have long term benefits and is it possible to pass it the next generation. The simple answers are yes and yes! Let's take a closer look at the final account.

In his old age, Abraham sent his trusted servant to find a bride for his son, Isaac. This caravan was composed of ten camels loaded with a dowry, a down payment on this bride to be. These ten camels carried jewelry, gold, silver, clothes and anything else in that day that would be precious to this special bride. But of more importance to us is the proposal of Eleazar to the selected bride:

> *The lord has blessed my master abundantly and he has become wealthy. He has given him sheep and cattle, silver and gold, menservants and maidservants, and camels and donkeys. My master's wife Sarah has borne him a son in her old age and he has given him everything he owns!* (Genesis 24:35)

Let's not forget his final epitaph:

> *Altogether, Abraham lived a hundred and seventy-five years. Then Abraham breathed his last and died at a good old age, an old man and full of years; and he was gathered to his people* (vs. 25:8-9).

The Message translation uses the word "happy"! The word "full" can also be translated as "blessed." What a way to finish this life...happy and blessed!

There is another tidbit of truth that has so often been overlooked in this family and their dynamics. Hidden in Genesis 25:9, "His sons Isaac and Ishmael buried him..." We can only surmise, but I believe there had been some kind of reconciliation between these two that allowed the family to be reunited in the end. They may have lived quite close to each other as the body of Abraham, by custom, would have been buried the day of death or not longer than a 24-hour period later.

Don't overlook the fact that Ishmael was the father of twelve sons who founded twelve tribal nations according to the promised blessing that God gave to Abraham.

The First Generation

> *As for Ishmael, I have heard you (Abraham): I will surely bless him; I will make him fruitful and will greatly increase his numbers. He will be the father of twelve rulers, and I will make him into a great nation* (Genesis 17:20-21).

The blessings and promises of God always have long life! Ishmael became the founder of the Arab world...Isaac of the Jewish people.

The Bible has answered our questions. The blessing was beneficial for a lifetime in the family of Abraham. The Bible also reminds us that God can and will take care of you too as you obey His directives. And finally, yes, the blessing of God can be passed on the next generation and the next and the next...even as far as the promised "thousand generations of those who love" the Lord! And "...he (Abraham) has given him (Isaac) everything he owns!" (Because he was the son of the promise.) What will be your legacy to your next generation?

TAKE AWAY TRUTH: If God has chosen an Abraham with all his strengths and weaknesses and used him to found a great nation, He can also use you and your family to be the foundation upon which you, with God's help, can also build a four-generation legacy!

FOUR

The Second Generation: Isaac and Rebekah, Jacob and Esau

Isaac has been called "The man whose birth caused a laugh!" Isaac is one of the very few times, in the Bible, in which God selected a name for a child and announced it before he was born. (There were others named by God, in the Old Testament. We have: Isaac, Ishmael, Solomon, Josiah, Cyrus, and Isaiah's son. In the New Testament, John the Baptist and Jesus Christ!)

Isaac was born when his dad was 100 years old and his mother was 90 or so. His beautiful name is translated as "God laughed," or "the laughing one," or even "he laughed," and likely, "he caused others to laugh." You get the idea. His birth commemorated the two laughings at the promise of God: the laugh of his dad who laughed so hard he was knocked off his feet and fell on his face (Genesis 17:17) and the laugh of his mother, Sarah, who laughed to herself and thought, "After I am worn out and my husband is old, will I now have this pleasure?" But God heard her laugh! What kind of a home this must have been with all this laughter going on! How did it effect the childhood of Isaac? Every time there was a visitor or stranger, the story of his being born and the laughter of his mom and dad and their guests must have made a wonderful, joyful, laugh-filled home for the child who was named, "God's laugh!"

Isaac was the child of the covenant of blessing. "I (God) will establish My covenant with him!" Note that this was the promise given to the three patriarchs in succession: To Abraham, as he left Chaldea (Genesis 12:3); to Isaac, when in Canaan during a nation-wide famine (Genesis 26:4); to Jacob at Bethel (Genesis 28:14). Isaac, however, was the first one to inherit the blessing covenant, and it was to him that God gave the whole total inheritance of Abraham (Genesis 24:35), setting the precedent for the others to follow.

We really have no record of Isaac's early life, other than after eight days he was circumcised. We can surmise that as a child he was made aware of the covenant of blessing of which he was to be the rightful heir. According to the historian, Josephus, Isaac would have been about 25 years old when his father took him from Beer-sheba to Moriah, where he was to be the burnt offering on the altar by Abraham. What must this have done to his psyche, to his thinking, to how it must have affected his life from that point on? It was a lesson in Abraham's unquestioning faith in God, but what about Isaac? I believe from that day on with his surrender to a likely death, that he became a very different, dedicated man.

It's important to note that Isaac was the first person to live his entire life with the blessing. Abraham was 75 when he began living with the blessing. Isaac lived with and under the blessing for 180 years!

Isaac was about thirty-six years old when his momma (Sarah) died and apparently grieved deeply over her death. There's nothing like a good wife to fill the vacancy left by Mom. The finding of a wife for him is one of the most romantic stories of the Bible. Genesis 26 makes an interesting and fun read. Let's take a couple of things from this ancient idyll, really one of the most beautiful you can find in history. To his credit, Isaac was the only one of the patriarchs who had but one wife for a lifetime. The other fact to take note of is that he left the choice of a wife up to God.

When the camel caravan came into sight bringing God's choice to him—what excitement! Isaac had been anxiously looking for the return of his servant with his future wife, and the indication is that he was out in the field meditating, or it could also be that he was in prayer for this choice in his life.

Isaac and Rebecca were childless for a number of years until God answered the prayers of Isaac on behalf of his wife because she was barren. "The Lord answered his prayer, and his wife Rebekah became pregnant" (Gen. 25:21).

It was another miracle baby, in fact two, and not an ordinary pregnancy because, The babies jostled each other within her, and she said, "Why is this happening to me?" and went to inquire of the Lord. Right here, this story takes a very interesting turn. Let's listen in on this word from the Lord,

> *The Lord said to her, "Two nations are in your womb, and two peoples from within you will be separated; one people will be stronger than the other, and the older will serve the younger!"* (Gen. 25:23)

Talk about setting up future conflicts that came out of this prophetic word from the Lord. Do you think this is the word that Rebekah had in mind when she gave God a hand to make sure this was fulfilled, when it came time for the birth-right blessing? The older would serve the younger? Very interesting. Later, one of the saddest verses about family life appears, "Isaac, who had a taste for wild game, loved Esau but Rebekah loved Jacob!" Talk about an all-time mess of a family life. Favoritism—how many families have been touched with this monster?

Isaac was about sixty years old when the twin boys were born. It also seems likely that he outlived Rebekah, but the last fifty or so years of his life he was nearly blind—a bit sad and maybe even pitiful for God's chosen one.

The character of Isaac is an interesting study—wonderful and beautiful yet flawed in many ways. Perhaps the most deceitful was a lesson learned from his Papa. He too lied about his relationship with his beautiful, gorgeous wife, like his father, when he was in hostile territory. He too was afraid for his own skin and lied when he said, "Rebekah is my sister!" Like father, like son! Not good. It seems that more than the blessing can be passed or modeled from one generation to the next. It's interesting that a heathen, ungodly king rebuked Isaac for this prevarication and not God who rebuked the wandering and fearful man.

Isaac also loved savory food. Meaning what? Was this a weakness of character? Was he a glutton? Was food more important to him than the relationship with his other son? Did he love food all out of proportion to more important issues of life? I don't know, but we can speculate.

In the matter of Esau and the blessing—at this point, was Isaac in rebellion against God's purposes for the future of his sons? Surely he knew about the prophecy given to Rebekah at their birth. What an interesting brew of good and not so good in the life of the second patriarch.

How about the positive side of his character? There are many commendable features that would have been modeled for his family and especially for his sons. Let's take another look. Much has been made about Isaac's submission to the will of his father as well as being submissive to his father's God.

- Physically, he was mature enough to have overcome an elderly father when told to lay upon the altar, but willingly he submitted. Theologians have gone so far as to hold up Isaac as the type of Christ in his submission. (Gen. 22:6,9)

- It also can be assumed that prayer and meditation were a

regular part of his lifestyle. Implied in this insight was his walk in the field, in the quiet of being alone with his God, was a daily practice. (Gen. 24:63)

- He had an instinctive trust in God. How had this become part of his life? This may have been because of this trait he had seen in the life of his father. (Gen. 22:7,9)

- He was a man who loved his wife with a deep devotion and a life-long loyalty. It's been said that the best thing a man can do for his kids is to love their mother. He sought comfort in the person of his wife. (Gen. 24:67)

- He was a man of peace...he sought peace...he wanted to live a life that was at peace with his neighbors. When conflicts arose he was the peacemaker. He was generous in working out conflicts. Also implied in this account is that his servants also believed in peace making. (Gen. 26:12-33)

- He was a man of worship, prayerfulness, and sacrifice. He built an altar, which is something of permanence... and called on the Lord! (Gen. 26:25a)

- He was a man who kept the priorities of his life in focus. He knew what was really important in life. Notice especially his choice of actions...he built an altar but pitched his tent and dug a well! Too many of us are "building" and "pitching" our family altars! There's a big difference between building and digging, and pitching a tent.

Pitching a tent is not permanent while building an altar is something permanent. (Gen. 26:25b)

- Don't get the wrong impression. Isaac was a man who was to be respected and envied and powerful enough so that all his neighbors wanted to be on his good side. Even though he was envied, they wanted a peace treaty with him. (Gen. 26:28-29)

- He was a man of faith! In fact, his faith was so great, it was listed in the "Hall of Faith." In faith he blessed the next generation! (Hebrews 11:16-20)

- He walked before God in such a way that this was recognized by his own son, Jacob. Not only that, he led his family in such a way that they too wanted the same walk with God. What a tribute, to live as a pattern for others to follow the same lifestyle. (Gen. 48:15-16)

- Isaac may well have had a special, intimate, godly relationship which was defined as "the fear of Isaac!" This fear of Isaac, again, was how he related to God. This example was also lived out in the life of his son, Jacob. (Gen. 31:42, 53)

The practical life-lessons from this life are fabulous! The manifestation of the power of the blessing in the life of Isaac rose to a new level after he submitted to Abraham on the altar. I believe that living a lifetime with the blessing manifested itself in new and different ways than in the life of his father, Abraham. This is a biblical pattern of living. The next generation should live better in all ways than their parents.

Just one more example. When famine came to the land of Israel during the life time of Abraham, he was forced to flee to Egypt for food and survival. However, when famine returned to the land in Isaac's life, God told him to stay in the land, and he and his family would be sustained. In fact God blessed him in such a way that when he planted his crops, he received a 100-fold, 100 times multiplication of his crops. It was such an evident blessing that it caused the Philistines to envy him.

After a period of years, Jacob, along with his wives and kids, returned to Mamre, which is in Hebron, to live near his father. They became a multi-generational family. It was here that Isaac died at the age of one hundred and eighty years and as the Bible says, "he was gathered unto his people" and a very important fact is that both of his sons, Esau and Jacob, buried him about 1881 B.C.

TAKE AWAY TRUTH: Isaac lived another fascinating life—a mix of good and bad. It gives hope to all of us that with our mix of flaws and positives, we can be used of God to build a generational legacy! Just as character was built into the life of Isaac, we can be used of God to build our own character and leave a legacy for the next generation to follow!

FIVE

The Third Generation: Jacob, Leah, Rachel, Bilhah, and Zilpah

Can you imagine what it must have been like to live in a family with eighteen people including the mamas, one papa, and thirteen kids?! Think of the dynamics and intrigue and agendas that must have been at work! What a story and what a family and what a father!

Abraham, the first generation, planted the seed and laid the foundation. Isaac, the second, watered the roots, nourished the tree, and kept it going. Jacob, the third generation grew the family tree, and did he ever!

Jacob is the second of a set of twins. Therefore he was known as the younger brother, even though born at virtually the same time. But remember that the birth order was a really big thing for this era in history. When the blessing was passed on by Isaac, it turned into one of the all-time family messes.

We can't blame Jacob entirely for the problem about the blessing. His parents played favoritism with disastrous results. I remind you once again about this tidbit of information, "Isaac loved Esau, but Rebekah loved Jacob!" (Gen. 25:28) And when it came time for the blessings to be passed to Jacob and Esau, Rebekah fouled it up. But give her credit, she may have believed God needed some help to make the earlier prophecy come to pass. Let's read it, The Lord said to her,

> *Two nations are in your womb, and two peoples from within you will be separated; one people will be stronger than the other, and the older will serve the younger* (Gen. 25:23).

How God would have made this come true we can only speculate, but we know of the deception that Rebekah practiced with the help of her favorite son. What do you think this set of lies and actions must have done to the psyche and soul and future of Jacob?

Mama and son stole the first blessing, the best blessing, the double-portion blessing. But the son, all by himself, had already stolen his brother's birthright (Gen. 25:29-34), so there you have a double, double-cross! (Traditionally, the double-portion blessing went to the first born son...so in the absence of the father, the eldest would also be able to sustain the mother and the rest of the family.) Of course, this caused problems. Isaac also blessed Esau with a lesser blessing. But don't forget that Isaac also gave Jacob another blessing, at the insistence of Rebekah, before Jacob fled for his life from the threats of his brother (Gen. 28:1-5). He went in search of a suitable wife in Paddan Aram to the home of crafty, nasty, deceitful good old uncle Laban. It was like jumping from the frying pan into the fire! Poor naïve Jacob, whose name means "the heel grabber" or "the supplanter," had met up with a real professionally nasty guy.

Jacob is the best biblical example of the presence and conflicts of two natures—a real life Dr. Jekyll and Mr. Hyde, as created in Robert Louis Stevenson's story. Jacob is both good and bad—when bad, he is really bad; and when good, really good. He is a character worth studying because of his strength and weakness. In spite of all of his failings, he was chosen by God to be a blessed person. In his life, there is hope for all of us because it's possible to turn a life around. He was a deceitful, dishonest man but became a man of prayer. The inconsistencies of his life are easy to see, yet he became a "prince with God" as he was re-named by Him.

Let's look a bit deeper and catch the good and bad, the black and white of this third generation of a legacy in the making.

- Don't forget that he was a victim of his mother's favoritism. Always keep this fact in mind as we work our way though his life. (Gen. 25:28)

- Jacob was a selfish man as shown to us in living color. He managed to steal his brother's birthright for a paltry, pitiful mess of stew! (Gen 25:31-34) He drove a hard one-sided bargain, but don't forget that the Bible also said that "Esau despised his birthright."

The Third Generation

- Jacob was crafty and deceitful and a polished, convincing liar and actor. What else? Isn't this enough? Where did he get this from? Most likely from his lovely and beautiful mother. Did he really have a conscience as he carried out the scheme of his mama in stealing the patriarchal blessing that should have gone to the eldest son? He deceived his blind father. He blatantly used the Lord's name in his lying. Martin Luther said about Jacob, "Had it been me, I would have dropped that savory dish of venison." Whatever he was or had become, he was proficient with his lying and acting. He fooled his own father!

- This sharp, crafty wheeler-dealer eventually mended his ways in meeting with God in two spiritual experiences—at Bethel and Peniel. These two events would change any of us. (Gen. 28:12-22; 32:22-32)

- Jacob had his romance spoiled and was more than paid back with the same coin of deception, which he had used on his brother and father. This time it was rascally Uncle Laban who switched brides on his wedding night! It was "weak-eyed, ugly" Leah, the older sister in place of the "lovely in form and beautiful" Rachel. But give him his due, in love and romance, he worked a total of 14 years to pay for his bride. What a story of love and deceit! (Gen. 29:14-30)

- Without a doubt, Jacob was industrious, hard working, a thinker, and a brilliantly smart man in his planning. He apparently developed new techniques for raising cattle, sheep, goats, and donkeys. (Gen. 29:14; 30:25-43)

- Jacob was a praying man...yet did he have a "daily" prayer life, or did he pray earnestly when faced with a difficult situation. The instances when he prayed were moments when he really needed God's help. (Gen. 32:9-12, 24-30)

- He was blessed with sons, twelve in fact, who became the foundation of an entire nation! Later this nation was spoken of as the "sons of Jacob" and later as "the children of Israel." (Gen. 48:49; Num. 24:19)

- Jacob was such a man of faith that he is listed among the members of the "Faith Hall of Fame" in the book of Hebrews. "By faith Jacob, when he was dying, blessed each of Joseph's sons, and worshiped as he leaned on the top of his staff" (Heb. 11:21).

- We must not forget the experience of Jacob as he wrestled with an angel or as Jacob stated, "I saw God face to face, and yet my life was spared!" He was changed forever...from being the schemer to now a "Prince with God!" From this day onward, he walked with a limp so all who saw him knew he was a changed man. Face to face with God and a daily walk with God. If Jacob could be changed, none of us are beyond a life change either!

Have you noticed, as we have worked our way through the lives of these three patriarchs that Jacob, his life, his wives, his foibles, and his strengths take up more of the

The Third Generation

biblical account than either Abraham or Isaac? Why? Is it because the third generation needs more attention, more emphasis, or just that God wanted to teach more lessons from his life than the previous? So today it's the God of Abraham, Isaac, and Jacob!

This is a man and his family who have impacted the world from that day to our present day! The blessings of the children of Jacob are still blessing the world beyond anything we could write in this short book. But think of the magnitude of this slice of history.

He blessed:

> *May the God before whom my fathers, Abraham and Isaac walked, the God who has been my shepherd all my life to this day, the Angel who has delivered me from all harm...may he bless these boys. May they be called by my name and the names of my fathers Abraham and Isaac, and may they increase greatly upon the earth!* (Genesis 48:15-16)

He blessed two grandsons, the sons of Joseph, and also predicted their future and made the same prophecy that was given to his mother at his birth:

> *In your name (God's name) will (the nation of) Israel pronounce this blessing "May God make you like Ephraim and Manasseh!"* (Genesis 48:17-20)

Today in Israel, this is the most often spoken blessing over boys. Many families make this their daily blessing in the morning as they prepare for the day and at evening at bed-time. But without fail, this blessing is prayed every

Sabbath, over their sons—the "children of Israel!" The blessing most frequently and regularly prayed over the girls of Jewish parents is: "May God make you as Sarah, Leah, Rebekah and Rachel!"

Then there were more blessings passed on by Jacob which began like this:

> *Then Jacob called for his sons and said: "Gather around so I can tell you what will happen to you in days to come, assemble and listen, sons of Jacob; listen to your father Israel"* (Genesis 49:1-2)

We should also note that of the twelve sons, Joseph was given another beautiful and much more detailed blessing which is well worth reading from Genesis 49:21-26.

These blessings are concluded:

> *All these are the twelve tribes of Israel, and this is what their father said to them when he blessed them, giving each the blessing appropriate to him* (Genesis 49:28).

After taking a good look at the life of Jacob, I can only come to the conclusion that the effects of the blessing on his life rose to a new level, beyond that of his father and grandfather. You might be thinking, *How can that be?* The argument I would make to back up that premise simply is to look closely at his life. Following the deceit to receive the blessing, he was forced to leave home and run for his life to get away from an angry brother. It seems as though he left home with nothing, then he found employment as a volunteer on Uncle Laban's ranch and worked the next fourteen years with no apparent monetary wage. It took those years to earn the right to marry two wives.

Jacob had so benefited Laban because when it came time for Jacob to leave with his wives and kids, Uncle Laban begged him to stay, "Name your wages, and I will pay them." But Laban has made a most interesting and beneficial reason to have Jacob stay when he said, "I have learned by divination that the Lord has blessed me because of you!" (Gen. 30:27-30) What a beautiful statement—God has blessed me because of you!

Jacob became wealthy and blessed in spite of the rascally, wily old Uncle Laban. "Your father (Laban) has cheated me by changing my wages ten times. However, God has not allowed him to harm me" (Gen. 31:4-9). Jacob left home penniless and returned to his homeland as a wealthy man.

One more slice of information tells us that Uncle Laban even passed on a blessing to his daughters and grandchildren: "Early the next morning Laban kissed his grandchildren and his daughters and blessed them" (Gen. 31:55).

We have not nearly gleaned all of the life lessons we can learn from this man, his family, his God, and his blessing. Read it again. Much can be learned in third generational living with the blessing and the covenants of God.

We have the knowledge that Jacob ran away from his

parents and home with nothing but his father's spoken blessings. How did Jacob in only twenty years have such abundance that he attempted to give some of it away to Esau? On the other hand, Esau also had such abundance that he didn't have room for more! What brought such abundance to these two brothers? The simple answer is that they were both blessed by their father.

But in Jacob's case, we have specific answers of how he lived this life with the blessing coupled with these four life principles.

- Jacob was a hard worker in good and bad times, whether it was too hot or too cold, he kept at it, perseverance marked his life. "This was my situation: The heat consumed me in the daytime and the cold at night, and sleep fled from my eyes. It was like this for the twenty years I was in your household" (Gen. 31:40-41).

- Jacob was loyal to his employer and stayed with his assignments, even when he was not treated fairly and even mistreated. "You know that I've worked for your father with all my strength, yet your father has cheated me by changing my wages ten times" (Gen. 31:6-7).

- Jacob was a man who knew how to focus, how to keep the big picture in mind, to not be deterred from his goals in life. We see this in his love for and devotion to wed the beautiful Rachel. Jacob was in love with Rachel and said, "I'll work for you for seven years in return for your younger daughter Rachel..." Laban replied, "It is not our

The Third Generation

custom here to give the younger daughter in marriage before the older one...Finish this daughter's bridal week; then we will give you the younger one also, in return for another seven years of work!" (Gen. 29:18, 25-26). Talk about dealing with disappointment, with a scheming rascal of an uncle. He worked fourteen years, with no pay check. His work took care of the dowry for these two daughters of Laban who became his wives. He did not give up!

- Jacob lived with the special generational blessing, the covenant of blessing through his father Isaac and his grandfather Abraham. Think of what has happened in his life when he combined the blessing with his stick-to-it-tiveness! Isaac blessed him and said: "May God give of heaven's dew and of earth's richness...an abundance of grain and new wine. May nations serve you and peoples bow down to you. Be lord over your brothers, and may the sons of your mother bow down to you. May those who curse you be cursed and those who bless you be blessed" (Gen. 27-29). Note that this was the first of the blessings given by his father. The second, and maybe even more meaningful and more powerful, was this:

> May God Almighty bless you and make you fruitful and increase your numbers until you become a community of peoples. May He give you and your descendants the blessing given to Abraham, so that you may take possession of the land where you now live as an alien, the land God gave to Abraham (Gen. 28:3-4).

These four principles: hard work, loyalty, determination, and walking, living, working, raising a family in a covenant blessing relationship with God can also release God's favor in your life and the life of your family! He was a highly motivated man with his vision, his dream and this may well have provided the motivation for this lifestyle. You may have been blessed with a wonderful heritage but we all must understand that God will not bless the work of a lazy person who is not consistent in fulfilling the plans and purposes of God.

The blessings of God in Jacob's life were evident to others, particularly Laban. Before Jacob entered this man's life, Laban likely had little by way of blessings. Again, I remind you, that in a short twenty years, Laban and Jacob were both enjoying the results of Jacob's hard work. I love the implications of this verse: "I have learned…that the Lord has blessed me because of you" (Gen. 30:27).

However, it seems as though Laban was not a prudent manager, saver, or investor—he didn't plan for the future. Leah and Rachel told Jacob that their father had squandered their inheritance, leaving them nothing.

I know that this concept is not "politically correct" in today's world, but we see how it worked in the life of Jacob. Leah and Rachel realized God's blessings were with their husband and knew they would not have to fear losing their inheritance or lifestyle. (Gen. 31:14-16)

There are many ways in which the blessings on Jacob multiplied beyond the level of either his grandfather,

Abraham, or his father, Isaac. There was a new level of the blessing as seen in the twelve branches on the family tree. It can be seen in the growth of fruit—the seed was planted, the trunk has grown, now the branches as well as the fruit of spiritual and material blessings can easily be seen.

TAKE AWAY TRUTH: What an amazing life story! More space has been given for us to see the big picture of a life with all the ups and downs as well as life disappointments. The largest truth is that if God can and will use a man like Jacob, God is more than willing to use all of us to make an impact on the next generation. We may not be there at the present, but with God's help, we too can make a huge difference in the people who follow us!

SIX

The Fourth Generation: The Children of Jacob

By Leah	By Rachel	By Bilhah	By Zilpah
Reuben (1st)	Joseph (12th)	Dan (5th)	Gad (7th)
Simeon (2nd)	Benjamin (13th)	Naphtali (6th)	Asher (8th)
Levi (3rd)			
Judah (4th)			
Issachar (9th)			
Zebulon (10th)			
Dinah (11th)			

What a family! This family has more than its share of sibling rivalry, birth order issues, favoritism, intrigue, competition, deceit, and other negative issues. On the other hand, there was loyalty, love, watching out for each other, protectiveness, honor, hard work, blessings, and much more on the positive side of life too.

Seventy now make up this family—there were twelve sons, their children, and their children's children. This now is the family, with all their positives and negatives, who will become the nation of Israel.

The Fourth Generation

Global famine changed everything, all their comfortable circumstances of living were upturned. In order to survive, Jacob was forced to move the entire family to Egypt in order to protect this family tree. Maybe in the life cycle of our families, there may also be a time to stay and a time to move—a time of plenty and perhaps a time of starvation. Jacob's sons were now the fourth generation from the founder, Abraham.

The fourth generation, more than any other, is faced with a unique problem that must be solved. Research will reveal to you that in any family business or family, this fourth generation is the most vulnerable in many ways. For example, this generation is the most critical if the legacy is going to live on. Too many family run businesses fail in this fourth group of great-grandchildren. Why? They are now far removed from the original vision or business dream. They get tired of the "same old...same old" and want something different. For example, they might wonder what was so special about great-grandpa that they have to keep up this boring business?

There's another word of warning—the same syndrome holds true for churches, religious institutions, denominations, educational systems, and even nations. Consider what happened in the life of Israel. Moses was the first generation that came out of Egypt, out of bondage, to experience an awesome deliverance. Joshua was the second generation, and his leadership was supported by elders who had also experienced the miraculous works and provisions of the Lord during the Exodus. Then came the fourth generation, and the lesson for our day,

> *After that whole generation had been gathered to their fathers, another generation grew up, who knew neither the Lord nor what He had done for Israel. Then the Israelites did evil in the eyes of the Lord and served the Baals. They forsook the Lord, the God of their fathers* (Judges 2:10-12).

This generation found themselves in apostasy, and you can read their sad story of a whole series of judges who continued this downward spiral and others who led them back to God and the teachings of the Torah. What a sad story.

Back to Jacob and his seventy strong—that fourth generation's greatest need was for protection! Jacob's family had to be preserved and protected from starvation. What about the fourth generations of our day? Look about, see the destruction of morals, values, character, and loyalties that are perpetuated on today's youth. The need for protection from these evils falls upon the elders again today.

This family legacy began with Abraham's seed. Isaac watered it until it became a trunk, Jacob provided the branches, and the twelve sons made the fruit possible. This story is contained in Genesis chapters twelve through fifty, the final chapter. The story of the nation begins with Abraham, ends with Moses, and is recorded as the Jewish legacy from the book of Exodus through Deuteronomy thirty-four. Today that legacy of Moses is celebrated often wherever and whenever the Torah is studied or read.

The Fourth Generation

The celebration of the Passover is an annual event in Israel's history. The roots and branches of this family tree continue to grow as the Gentile branches have also become part of this fabulous story. Paul, the apostle of the New Testament, reminds us that we now "share in the nourishing sap from the olive root, do not boast over those branches. If you do, consider this: you do not support the root, but the root supports you!" (Romans 11:17-18)

Some years ago, a reporter covering the conflict in Sarajevo saw a little girl shot by a sniper. The back of her head had been partially blown away. This reporter threw down his pad and pencil and recorder and stopped being a reporter. He rushed to the man who was holding the child and helped them both into the front seat of his car. As the reporter raced to the hospital, the man holding the bleeding child said, "Hurry, my friend. My child is still alive." A few moments later he said, "Hurry, my friend. My child is still breathing." They continued the race with death.

Another moment passed, he said, "Hurry, my friend. My child is still warm." Finally, "Hurry. Oh my Lord, my child is getting cold."

By the time they arrived at the hospital, the little girl had died. As the two men were in the bathroom, washing the blood off their hands and clothes, the man turned to the reporter and said, "This is a terrible task for me. I must go tell the father that his child is dead. He will be heartbroken."

The reporter was amazed and looked at the grieving man and said, "I thought she was your child."

The man looked back and said, "No, but aren't they all our children?"

Those who are little and helpless and those who suffer in reality belong to all of us and if we care about this next generation we will respond! It's time to get really serious about our next generation. It's time that we decide what really is important in our lives.

Sam Nunn, former U.S. Senator, in a speech given at the National Prayer Breakfast in Washington, D.C. said: "Intellectual honesty, moral and ethical behavior, we must decide what is important."

So, we have completed our look at the original four generation legacy of the covenant blessing. It's been an exciting journey. Now in the next chapter we will explore how we as twenty-first century inhabitants, build a four generation legacy. And let's move on to look at God's plans for your family. What is important when it comes to the next generation?

TAKE AWAY TRUTH: It is still possible to build a four-generation legacy in the twenty-first century world with God's help! If it happened once, it can happen again with God's help! If Abraham, Isaac and Jacob did it, you can too.

SEVEN

The Generational Covenant Blessing

He remembers His covenant forever, the word He commanded, for a thousand generations, the covenant He made with Abraham, the oath he swore to Isaac. He confirmed it to Jacob as a decree, to Israel as an everlasting covenant. To you I will give the land of Canaan as the portion you will inherit! (Psalm 105:8-11)

How do we intentionally build a culture, a value system, a moral system, a family system, and day-to-day principles that will allow us to build a four-generation legacy? The how-to-do-it is hidden in the Torah, and the rest of the Bible.

In our Gentile (non-Jewish) world, business is conducted and made possible because of agreements called contracts, treaties, mortgages, pledges, vows, pacts, bargains, promissory notes, and agreements. However, in the ancient world and cultures the word covenant is understood to be more than an agreement because it was sealed with blood. Thus we have the biblical covenant of the Hebrews directly connected with the blood of the participants. A covenant could also be sealed with a meal. Before we proceed further, let's take a deeper look so that we can understand what the covenant of blessing is all about and the history of how it came into practice.

The first covenant in the Bible was between Noah and God that would save his life and that of his family during the flood. This covenant was also made with the future inhabitants that there would never be another worldwide flood. The sign that confirmed this covenant with the rest of the world is seen by all of us in the form of a rainbow—a covenant that has lived for the "thousand" generations that God so often speaks of, a confirmation for all the world to see every time it rains and the sun shines.

The second covenant was confirmed between God and Abram. At age seventy-five, Abram began following this promise, in fact this covenant was progressively revealed during this life journey as well as the plans God had for Abram's future family.

- GOD said: "I will make you into a great nation and I will bless you" (Genesis 12:2).

- GOD said: "As for Me, this is my covenant with you: You will be the father of many nations. No longer will you be called Abram; your name will be Abraham, for I have made you a father of many nations" (Genesis 17:4).

- GOD said: "I will make you very fruitful; I will make nations of you, and kings will come from you. I will establish my covenant as an everlasting covenant between Me and you and your descendants after you for the generations to come, to be your God and the God of your descendants after you" (Genesis 17:6-7).

- GOD said: "Abraham will surely become a great and powerful nation, and all nations on earth will be blessed through him. For I have chosen him, so that he will direct his children and his household after him to keep the way of the Lord" (Genesis 18:18).

- GOD said: "I will surely bless you and make your descendants as numerous as the stars in the sky and as the sand on the seashore. Your descendants will take possession of the cities of their enemies, and through your offspring all nations on earth will be blessed, because you have obeyed Me" (Genesis 22:17-18).

Notice something very important in this progression. With each act of obedience, God increased the far-reaching effects and magnitude of His promises. They went from just plain "nation" to becoming a "great nation" then to "nations of kings" and finally to a nation that would be blessing to the "entire world!" Do not forget the key to these promises made: Obedience to the demands that God had commanded!

The Abrahamic Covenant

All of the biblical covenant blessings are possible because of the link to the Abrahamic covenant! Abraham discovered and was given the major "secret" in the covenant:

The Lord confides in those who fear Him; He makes His covenant known to them (Psalm 25:14).

The Hebrew word translated as "covenant" is "b'rit," and it can be found some 280 times the Old Testament. The real, powerful secret is that all covenants are linked to a blood sacrifice. And this was a secret that had been hidden by God from Abraham for about twenty-four years. The final sealing of this covenant was by the shedding of blood.

B'rit implies that making a covenant involves a "cutting," a ceremony in which two persons come together and cut covenant. When Abraham and God "cut covenant," it involved Abraham bringing a heifer, a female goat, a ram, a turtle dove, and a young pigeon as offerings. Abraham then divided the larger animals into halves. Here's how the Bible records this ceremony, When the sun had set and darkness had fallen, a smoking firepot with a blazing torch appeared and passed between the pieces (this was a "theophany"—an appearance of God). On that day the Lord made a covenant with Abraham and said, "To your descendants I give this land" (Gen. 15:17-18). This sacrifice and the shedding of blood confirmed it!

In many other parts of the world, blood covenants have been used for centuries. As an example, Dr. David Livingston, the noted and famous missionary to Africa, witnessed many covenant rites while in Africa. He also made a "blood" covenant with Queen Manenko of the Balonda tribes. In many instances, an incision was made in

The Generational Covenant Blessing

the wrist and rubbed with gunpowder creating a sign that could easily be seen and felt by others. Most often when hands were shaken, the wrist was turned to show that perhaps the person you are meeting was in covenant relationships.

The implications were that you were not only dealing with a single person, you also were dealing with others so you had better be careful of how you would deal with this person. In today's language, we'd say that someone else had our back covered. If this covenant was broken in any way, the chief pronounced curses on the person who broke the covenant. Both parties exchanged gifts as part of these rituals or rites.

In 1871, Henry Stanley traveled to Africa searching for Livingston. He happened to encounter the most feared tribal leader who controlled more than ninety thousand square miles of territory. Stanley had been warned to avoid this leader, named Mirambo, but came across this chieftain on April 22, 1876. They agreed to make a "strong friendship." Once this covenant was ratified, the entire tribe became friends with the chieftain's new covenant partner. Every inch of the land controlled by the chieftains was now open for travel without danger to Stanley, the chieftain's new friend, as a result of the covenant. Stanley wrote that his arm was used to draw blood fifty times to "cut" covenant with tribal leaders in Africa! (H. Clay Trumbull, *The Blood Covenant,* Impact Books, Joplin, MO, 1975, p. 6, 10, 16-17)

So what does all this blood letting have to do with us who are living in the 21st century? Often the tribal chief would send a representative to shed his blood on behalf of the chief. This gives us a vivid image of making a new covenant that affects all of us:

> *For God so loved the world that He gave his one and only Son, that whoever believes in Him shall not perish but have eternal life* (John 3:16).

Jesus Christ was that Son who became God's representative. He used His own blood to redeem us, to make an everlasting covenant between us and God so that we who have been redeemed have access to God the Father.

> *He (Christ) did not enter by means of the blood of goats and calves; but He entered the Most Holy Place once for all by his own blood, having obtained eternal redemption. The blood of goats and bulls and the ashes of a heifer sprinkled on those who are ceremonially unclean sanctify them so that they are outwardly clean. How much more, then, with the blood of Christ, who through the eternal Spirit offered himself unblemished to God, cleanse our consciences from acts that lead to death, so that we may serve the living God. For this reason Christ is the mediator of a new covenant, that those who are called may receive the promised eternal inheritance* (Hebrews 9:12-15).

Absolutely awesome!

I have taken this time so that we can understand some of the background and price that was paid to enter into the Abrahamic covenant of blessing for each and every one of

The Generational Covenant Blessing

us and the generations to follow. The sacrifice of Jesus Christ for us makes the blessing come alive!

The covenant could also be sealed by other means for the descendants of Abraham. There was the rite of circumcision on the eighth day after a boy's birth. This is most interesting in that the Jewish tradition, there is belief that the first seven days of an infant's life represents God's creation of the world in seven days. The number eight and the eighth day represents a new beginning. This brings the child into the covenant of Abraham. Also a new-born was to experience the celebration of one Sabbath before being circumcised. In America, if circumcision is chosen, it's usually at the request of the parents and is performed within two days of birth. However, the Torah-keeping Jews keep the command of God, "This is My covenant which you shall keep...He who is eight days old among you shall be circumcised, every male child in your generations..." (Gen. 17:10-12).

Even more interesting is that medical research has discovered two blessings linked to the Jewish pattern of circumcision. The *British Journal of Cancer* (19, no. 2, June 1965, 217-226) reported that certain cancers of the cervix appear lower in Jewish women in Israel than among other ethnic groups of women. It's strongly suggested that circumcision assists in preventing cervical cancer in Jewish women. Secondly, there is the blood clotting feature, vitamin K, that contains "prothrombin" (based on research) that is found on the eighth day after birth. An infant has more vitamin K available at that time than on any other day of his life, making the eighth day the best time for circumcision! God knew the medical and physical significance of an eight-day circumcision!

A covenant could also be sealed with a meal. The first covenant meal was served by Melchizedek, the first king and priest of Salem (Jerusalem), to Abraham in celebration of his victory over five kings. The second covenant meal mentioned in the Bible took place when Isaac had Esau prepare a last meal prior to receiving his father's blessing. Rebekah, the mama, realized this was a covenant blessing meal and prepared the meal and gave it to Jacob to deliver to his father so he could steal Esau's blessing. What an all time mess that was! Later, Jacob and his father-in-law, Laban, sealed their covenant by eating a meal on a pile of rocks as a memorial for future generations.

The most important covenant meal for the Jewish people took place after God had given His Ten Commandments on Mount Sinai. This meal sealed the deal between the Hebrew nation and God (Exodus 24:3-6, 10-11).

In our Christian celebrations, the Lord's Supper, the Last Supper, or the Communion meal, represents the body and blood of the Lord of Jesus Christ and makes a spiritual bond between the Lord and us, sealing the confidence and faith we have in the new covenant. This is our covenant meal, a perfect picture of the completion of the covenant made possible by the perfect sacrifice of Jesus Christ.

The Generational Covenant Blessing

In studying covenants there are at least three things that you will discover to be found in each: 1) Agreements are made between at least two parties. Our agreements with God are based on His written words (the Bible) which is His side. Our side is when we agree to live by and follow the teachings established in the New Testament. 2) Every covenant has conditions. As we read through the Bible, God continually reminds us like this: "If you will _____ (fill in the blank)...then I (God) will _____ (write in God's promise)." It's like the marriage agreement and conditions "for better, for worse, for richer, for poorer, in sickness and in health..." The conditions are sealed with a kiss, and the marriage is consummated during the honeymoon. 3) Every covenant has promises that are made to be kept. If Abraham's offspring followed the agreement made by Abraham and God to mark their sons, then God would bless them with favor, land, protection, prosperity, and blessings, and make them great.

Before we leave the covenant promises, one more feature must be noted. After his special covenant meal with Melchizedek, Abraham reaffirmed his covenant and gave a tenth (tithe) of all his goods to Melchizedek. This was so significant it was mentioned by the writer of Hebrews this way:

> *Without doubt the lesser person is blessed by the greater. In the one case, the tenth is collected by men who die; but in the other case, by him who is declared to be living. One might even say that Levi, who collects the tenth, paid the tenth*

through Abraham, because when Melchizedek met Abraham, Levi was still in the body of his ancestor (Hebrews 7:7-10).

Abraham set the pattern for his future generations to tithe of their herds, agriculture products, and financial incomes for God's blessings to be upon them personally and nationally.

So what has all of the above to do with the fourth generation? This blessing produced a nation composed of twelve great grandsons—a nation that was blessed and is still blessed down to our day. They had a great beginning. But as we began this chapter we had a problem: there is a responsibility of and to and for this fourth generation to protect the family tree. In our modern twenty-first generation, we have the same need. The fourth generation is likely the most critical if the family is to succeed beyond this point. Studies from the world of industry and family run businesses indicate that this is the most critical point of survival. More successful family businesses are lost in the fourth generation than in any other. Why? It can be contributed to as many factors as there are businesses. However, I believe that the third/fourth generations are the most vulnerable because they are so far removed from the original vision of the founder; and that vision, unless it is renewed and re-invigorated, dies by being sold or divided.

Therefore as we look ahead to the fourth generation, it requires a special focus to do what is right and positive so

The Generational Covenant Blessing

that your legacy will survive and grow beyond this fourth generation. This fourth generation became nation builders! So now, this may be the time to ask you the following: in which generation do you see yourself—first? second? third? or the fourth?

In the history of the world, there was only one "first" generation family—Adam and Eve! Abraham, in this book, is designated as the first generation. However, he had parents, grandparents, great-grandparents and even great-great-grandparents. He is considered the first because he began a new family, a family different from the world's kind of a family. His family was visited by God to create a new nation, to be the fountainhead from which all the world would be blessed. Therefore, Abraham biologically was a first, second, third, and fourth generation just like all the rest of us!

Even though God and His Word refer to generations, God has *no* grandchildren! He has only children. In other words, each person is to have a personal father-to-child relationship with God. Each person and each generation has the same privilege of being a first generation with new beginnings and the opportunity of establishing something new and special with God's help. And at the same time, in our family relations we are second, third, fourth, and more generational people.

Let me put it this way—no matter which generation you may be, we all must have a personal relationship with God the heavenly Father that has been made possible because of His only Son who provided the way to eternal life. No matter what generation I may be, I must honor and be mentored by previous generations. I must then be responsible to the generations that follow after me by being an example, mentoring, laying good foundations, and leaving a meaningful legacy for those who follow. This is an unending chain of people repeating this process over and over until we leave this world. One of my concerns is that I do not want to be a weak link in this chain of grace. I need to live and walk in such a way as to leave a clean path to follow with meaningful signposts along the way. We only have one chance at getting this right! There are no excuses, we cannot be re-born in the physical sense, but we can be born again in the spiritual sense. So there is a possible chance to start all over again.

TAKE AWAY TRUTH: We should be constantly concerned about getting this generational thing right this time, through our lifespan. None of us has been promised more than one life, and it must always be lived forward. There is no going back for another try at getting it right. Therefore, today is the day to get it right, to do our best with no regrets. Perhaps this is the moment for each of us to pause, think, and ask forgiveness from a loving heavenly Father, and to recommit, refocus, and keep on building a present generation in such a way for the next generation to also be mentored so they can carry on this multi-generation task!

EIGHT

Your Family Legacy

A good man (and woman) leaves an inheritance for their children's children (Proverbs 13:22a, paraphrased).

The Jewish four-generational pattern we have been looking at has been a fabulous guide to give us something to seriously think about. The word that comes to mind as we build our own legacy is intentional! It's a focus on a plan, a purpose, a reason for legacy concepts.

We have discovered this pattern as it began with Abraham and Sarah in what is called The Blessing, which became a covenant that sealed the Jewish people as a nation of destiny. Later it was sealed with the shed blood of Jesus Christ's suffering so that we, today, in the twenty-first century can also be a part of this covenant blessing. We must understand that the Jew and us (Gentiles)—Jews and the Church—all come from the same tree, the same roots, the same trunk, and the same branches. Here's the promise that makes our blessing a reality:

> *Christ redeemed us from the curse of the law by becoming a curse for us...He redeemed us in order that the blessing given*

to Abraham will come to the Gentiles through Christ Jesus, so that by faith we receive the promise (Galatians 3:13-14).

Based upon what we have just read, what should be included in a meaningful four generation legacy?

Looking at the long-term picture, please give consideration to the following three things:

A HERITAGE: Don't think in material terms yet. This should be customs, traditions, family kinds of things that need to be handed down to the next generations.

A LEGACY: This should be understood as passing a good name, a good reputation, and something useful to the next generation.

A DYNASTY: Think of this as being a succession of the family line. Passing the power that is maintained in a family to the next generation.

Now let's expand on each of the above. Understand that the following is by no means complete or a must for you. These are meant to be guidelines, suggestions, and concepts that can be easily grasped and understood by the next generations. Later, you will be challenged to make up your own plan, your own concepts, your special family traditions that no one else may think of.

The Family Heritage

A heritage is "something that comes or belongs to a person by reason of birth; something reserved for one; the heritage of the righteous; any property, especially land, that devolves by right of inheritance" (*Random House Dictionary*). Let's also think in terms such as a legacy, bequest, estate, bestowal, or birthright. What then should specifically included when thinking of a family heritage?

- LEAVE A SPIRITUAL LEGACY: This is your history of your walk with God, it's viewed as "His" story in you life as you have lived it and are living it out. It's the blessings you have experienced and received in your life. It's your day by day Christian living so your off-spring can see your love for the Lord by the actions of your life. It's your faithfulness in church attendance, acts of kindness toward others. It's an example of a life-style that is modeled before your next generation. Tell the stories of your personal experiences and blessings of God that you have seen and experienced. How about regular prayer times, Bible reading on a consistent basis, family devotions, and how others are respected and many more. Write you own list.

- LEAVE A REAL LIFE EXAMPLE OF INTEGRITY: Our world is quickly becoming a place were there are no boundaries, or moral values, no black and white, no more rights and wrongs, no more "thus saith the Lord" and everything is a mushy mishmash of political correctness. There is no better place to live a life of integrity than in the life laboratory of our homes! Today's society is short of integrity and honesty in all phases of life and living. Living it out falls directly to us so we have a positive expression of integrity in all of our life circumstances to leave behind. Integrity even if it is painful and even if no one is around to see an action. Remember, little eyes and ears don't miss a thing. This is a life quality you cannot finesse. This is demonstrated in what you do...not in what you say!

- **LEAVE AN EXAMPLE OF UNCONDITIONAL LOVE:** There might be a whole lot of misses and a few hits...ups and downs...good and bad...misunderstandings...but love covers a multitude of sins. If your progeny knows that no matter what happens in life and living...that your love is unconditional, life can go on. Forgiveness and grace make it possible to keep on trucking. This must be a constant in every family situation! This does not preclude actions of tough love, either! "Greater love has no one than this...that a person lays down a life for others!"

- **LEAVE LOTS OF PICTURES AND GOOD MEMORIES:** Our oldest son and his family, recently, experienced the total, I mean total, destruction of their home in a four-alarm fire. In a matter or minutes and short hours, they managed to save only themselves, their house pets and the clothes on their backs. That's all. No life was lost, but one of their most painful losses were their pictures and memory books and journals and logs. Irreplaceable. With today's many technologies, this is easier to do. But do not only create them...store a back-up in a fire-proof cabinet, safe or in digital cloud storage. Pictures can identify family members to other generations whom they may never have met. Each picture conjures up good memories.

- **LEAVE SOMETHING OF A FINANCIAL LEGACY:** Again, I remind you of this admonition: "A good man leaves an inheritance for his children's children" (Prov. 13:22). Yes...don't forget your own children, either. Most of us have only modest means and can only do a little something. Others of us have enough wealth to leave a continuous legacy in funding your home church, Bible schools, hospitals, foundations for good, orphanages, vital ministries, rehab centers and so on. Such are these legacies that produce ongoing rewards as they change lives for the better. Make sure you have a strong will, even better is a family trust or a foundation. (Please make sure you have used some professional help so that this is done in such a way that the government does not get it all. Know what I mean? Yes. Good. Just a word to the wise.)

Are you getting this concept? This suggested list is only the beginning of what you can do! Add to it, make it personal, make it in such a way as to reflect your life values that must be passed on to the next generations!

The Family Legacy

A legacy is different than heritage. Perhaps it is a subtle difference so that important aspects do run together. Here is how it is defined by *Random House College*

Dictionary: "By law, a gift of property, as money, by will, a bequest. Anything handed down from the past, as from an ancestor, or predecessor..." You can also think in the following terms: tradition, gift, inheritance, leftover, remaining portion, carry-over, throwback, transmission, heirloom, birthright, and hand-me-downs! Let's get specific with the following...

- LEAVE A FAMILY HERITAGE: As an example, I am a third generation minister, and my second son is a fourth generation minister. My grandfather was a lay minister, my father was a full time pastor, I have spent my life as a pastor, and now my son is a pastor, and it looks as though we also might have at least one or more ministers in our next generation of family heritage. On my wife's side of the family, music is the thing. Her parents were musicians and played in a group for barn dances, then in churches, Donna has served as a music director in churches, her brother spent his entire service in the Army band, two sons and a daughter are musicians, and now our grandchildren are musicians. It doesn't mean everybody has to follow in the same interest or occupations, but you get the idea. Honor the traditions that have been built around such interests. Build lasting memories!

- LEAVE SOMETHING OF MATERIAL VALUE: Legacies are built generation after generation when a name brand such as General Motors, Coca Cola, McDonalds, or a

Walmart continue to have successes from generation to generation. People tend to vividly remember two things about you—your dramatic entrance and your exit out of this life. Births and deaths are celebrated as are first impressions and last impressions. Think in terms of passing some material things that you have treasured and likely will or can be used by the next generation. You may have a special collection, homes, autos, machinery, jewelry, land, property, a family business, art, or writings, for example.

- **LEAVE A GOOD NAME:** This may be the most important thing to leave to the following generations. There is nothing more positive for the future of others than to carry a good name, a name that has been tested over the years, a name that has not been blemished, a name that has been built well, and a name that has finished the life journey well!

Solomon wrote: "An inheritance gained hastily at the beginning will not be blessed at the end" (Proverbs 20:21). Moses almost lost his legacy because he lost his temper and struck the rock and was not allowed into the Promised Land! David had a dark mark with his affair with Bathsheba and the murder of her husband. But he did repent and died as "the man after God's own heart." Peter would likely have ruined his future with his cursing and denying that he knew Jesus Christ. Samson broke all his Nazarite vows but did repent and was mentioned in the New Testament in the Book of Hebrews. These examples are important for us. None of us is perfect, but we can all leave a good name and a heritage that is beneficial to those who come behind us.

I am very much aware that kids and grandkids would rather have a pile of cash or a new car or the latest technological toy or just plain more stuff. We must be the parent and let them know that there are greater things to leave them than more earthly possessions or mere things that quickly fade in importance!

The Family Dynasty

I am not attempting to split hairs or draw fine lines of distinction because this concept of a legacy is spread over heritage, legacy, and the dynasty. There are differences that I am challenging you to give some serious thought to. A dynasty is: "A sequence of rulers or leaders from the same family, stock, or group" (*Random House Dictionary*). Perhaps this family concept has never been a focus of yours. A dynasty should be thought of in the following: A ruling house, a regime, lineage, administration, dominion, authority, or even as a jurisdiction. Governments think and function in such terms, why not you and your family?

- **LEAVE A SUCCESSION OF LEADERS:** You are all of the same stock or family. Why not mentor and train family leaders, community leaders, church leaders, industry leaders, political leaders, or educational leaders? Others are doing it intentionally! Why not you? Think about it. Leadership is not necessarily something people are born with; it's something that can be learned. Create leaders with positive outlooks on life, people whose value system is Bible based, people who can make a difference for the good in our world! Begin thinking in terms of succession. Others are; why not you?

- **LEAVE AN UNDERSTANDING OF POWER:** Power that can be used to create something wonderful and good and uplifting and positive for a family and a hurting world. Think of people who are powerless. Can they provide you with a job? Are they creators of wealth? Are they inventors of a better future?

  Power can be derived from a number of sources. Wealth can bring you power; education can be a power base; creativity is a source; inventions give you a voice in the public arena; a good name gives you power. Power, which is not to be abused, will also give you some control over your future life and the life of the next generation. Prayer can be a source of power; a strong Christian witness gives you power to influence others in a positive sense.

- **LEAVE AN UNBROKEN DYNASTY:** It's too easy to break a dynasty. They can be interrupted when a leader in this line of succession messes up: When a leader has publicly destroyed their integrity; when a leader brings disgrace on the family name, business, or heritage. The public examples are too numerous to enumerate here. But all of us have watched in fascination and horror as churches, institutions, universities, politicians, nations, and societies have collapsed because of failure in leadership. It is so important that we begin well but maybe even more important that we end well. Don't mess it up for the next generation.

Your Name

You got it from your father and your mother,
    it was all they had to give,
So it's yours to use and cherish for as long as you may live.
If you lose the watch they gave you,
    it can always be replaced.
But a black mark on your name, Son, Daughter,
    can never be erased.
It was clean the day you took it,
    and a worthy name to bear,
When they got it from their parents
    there was no dishonor there.
So make sure you guard it wisely, after all is said and done,
You'll be glad your name is spotless when you give it to
    your son or daughter!

—*(Perry Stone,* Breaking the Jewish Code, *Charisma House, Lake Mary, FL 32746, 2009, modified to reflect a family, not only a "father" in narrative, and changed the title, page 232)*

Your Current Legacy—a Blessing or a Curse?

All of us are living and leaving a legacy that may be good or bad. Whether we like it or not, the past cannot be erased because it's already written in stone. What we do from this moment on is of absolute importance to leaving a meaningful legacy for those who follow in our footsteps.

Perhaps the above has been a gentle reminder of the importance of a good legacy, or this may have been in indictment of your actions. Why do some people seem to be blessed and others are simply going from one mess up to another?

- **If you have messed up the past**: Are you familiar with the biblical concept of redemption, repentance, and God's grace? You can have a new beginning! Jesus gave his life as a blood sacrifice so that all of us can ask for forgiveness, repent of the past, make restitution, and start all over again. Jacob found forgiveness for his actions and moved under the blessing of God. Samson asked forgiveness and is recorded in the New Testament record as being a man of faith. David was able to start over as acknowledging his wrong actions and went on to be described by God as being "a man after God's own heart." Peter found forgiveness and went on to follow the Lord.

  Perhaps you are that person or family in need of a spiritual "blood transfusion" through the power of the new blood covenant. The past can be erased and forgiven, and it's possible to begin all over again. You can ask forgiveness of the family members you may have treated wrongly and together lay a new foundation. Be another Abraham and be the founder of a new legacy!

- **What if you have formed bad habits?** Habits are formed one action at a time. Poor habits lead to a poor, lousy lifestyle. Many have excused bad habits with a rationalization that goes something like this: "My grandpa was a lazy man, so my dad was really lazy, therefore I am a lazy man. My grandmother was a smoker, my mama was a two-pack-a-day smoker, and therefore my lungs are being destroyed because I am a three-pack-a-day smoker and I can't break the habit." It's time to break with the past! Lousy habits can lead to a lousy, rotten lifestyle. It's time to woman up and man up and be the mentor and start laying down a straight path!

A boy and his father were walking in the new fallen snow. The dad challenged the son to a contest, a contest to see who could walk the straightest path with their footprints in the fresh snow. The dad said, "See those two little trees on top of that ridge...you walk to the one of the left, and I'll walk to the one on the right. Let's see who walks the straightest path."

They set out, the little boy was looking down so as to plant his feet carefully. When they arrived on the ridge top and looked back, the boy's path was very crooked, but the dad's path was in an almost perfectly straight line. The son remarked, "Dad, how did you do it?"

It was another teachable moment. His father replied, "Son, you looked down at your feet, but I looked at my goal—the tree—kept my eye on the goal and never looked down as I walked."

- **What if you are caught up in wrong thinking?** Stinking thinking leads to a stinking lifestyle. Too many of us need a check-up from the neck-up! Stinking thinking eventually leads you into making smelly decisions! Napoleon Hill who wrote the book, *Think and Grow Rich*, quoted philosopher Will James who said: "A person by changing his or her thoughts can change their world." And James went on to claim this was the greatest discovery of the twentieth century.

Do you think it may also work in the twenty-first century as well? Your thought life is one thing over which you have control. And it's not enough to think about it, this thinking challenges all of us with these biblical thoughts on how to do it, for today and every day to come:

> *Your attitude should be the same as that of Christ Jesus! Finally, brothers, whatever is true, whatever is noble, whatever is right, whatever is pure, whatever is lovely, whatever is admirable...if anything is excellent or praiseworthy...think about such things! Whatever you have learned or received or heard from me, or seen in me... put into practice! And the God of peace will be with you!* (Philippians 2:5; 4:8-9)

It's time to create a new habit of thoughts in your life, refocus—correct thinking leads to correct living!

- **What if you are trapped in wrong relationships?** Living with toxic kinds of relationships can easily become a slippery slope that can pull or push you into the slime and muck of life. Do you have any kinds of friends or relatives that you should avoid? It's not a new life problem! It's as old as the hills and they are old, old. For example…what if Delilah was your hair stylist, like Samson had? What if a hottie like Bathsheba was your personal trainer in your local gym, and she took a shower in front of you as in David's life? What if you had a wife who looks back as in the case of Lot? Would you have hired Judas to be your family or company CFO or CPA? Or like Joseph who had the wife of Potiphar as well as Pharoah to be your boss? People like these are to be avoided! Or it may be that some of your "friends" or even some family members are to be avoided! It may not be easy, but it may be necessary!

The Bible offers hope:

> *At one time we too were foolish, disobedient, deceived and enslaved by all kinds of passions and pleasures. We lived in malice and envy, being hated and hating one another. But when the kindness and love of God our Savior appeared, He saved us, not because of righteous things we have done, but because of His mercy. He saved us through the washing of rebirth and renewal by the Holy Spirit, whom He poured out on us generously through Jesus Christ our Savior, so that,*

having been justified by His grace, we might become heirs having the hope of eternal life (Titus 3:3-7).

Don't miss the important words and their meaning: kindness, love, saved, rebirth and renewal and hope of eternal life! That's exactly what we need! We can't do it by ourselves; here's outside help! Our bad relationships can be changed until we are no longer trapped! My dad used to say: "It's easier to pull someone down than to lift them up to your level." There is good news! Here's another command: "Do not conform any longer to the pattern of this world, but be transformed by the renewing of your mind..." (Romans 12:2).

If you have messed up, have been caught in stinking thinking or trapped in wrong relationships...there is hope and help, grace and mercy. Through your obedience and turning around you too will experience the favor and blessing of God that is released to you through your obedience to God and His Word! You can be the catalyst of change in your life and legacy!

- **What if you do not have a family with which to build a lasting legacy?** If you have not been blessed with children, or you may have been living a single life, or if you are widowed or a widower, whatever your circumstances might be that you are left alone does not mean you are let off the hook of building a legacy! Christianity is all about mentoring others! You are responsible to also build a lasting legacy!

Choose someone or some others to whom you can pass your legacy to the next generation! Paul the Apostle apparently did not have a spouse or family, and look at the fantastic legacy he left behind—he mentored Timothy, Barnabas, John Mark, Priscilla, and many more. In fact, today we are all a part of his legacy. He wrote letters that are recorded as a major part of the New Testament. Jesus Christ had no spouse and no biological children, yet we have all been mentored by His life legacy. Both Elijah and Elisha apparently had no biological kids; however, Elijah mentored Elisha, and Elisha mentored the school of the prophets and more. Make this selection a matter of prayer and do it intentionally! There are many avenues through which you can leave something very meaningful.

TAKE AWAY TRUTH: It is possible for every one of us to build a four-generation legacy with God's help! There are no plausible, believable excuses for not doing it. The bottom line is that all of us are leaving a legacy—good, bad, or indifferent. The challenge is to build a positive, lasting legacy intentionally!

NINE

How Do We Build Our Legacy?

By faith Abraham, even though he was past age...was enabled to become a father.
By faith Isaac blessed Jacob and Esau in regard to their future.
By faith Jacob, when he was dying, blessed each of Joseph's sons, and worshiped...
By faith Joseph, when his end was near, spoke about the exodus of the Israelites from Egypt and gave instructions about his bones.
By faith Moses...was looking ahead to his reward.
                    (Hebrews 11:11, 20-24-26)

About the time of Christ's birth, Rabbi Jesus ben Sirach wrote for posterity: "The blessing of the father builds houses for the sons and daughters; the blessing of the mother fills them with good things."

In the Hebrew culture and the Old Testament, there was and is a marked tendency to favor blessing sons instead of daughters. However, in the New Testament, Jesus corrected this oversight when they "brought young children (boys and girls) to Him and He took them up in

His arms, put His hands on them, and blessed them" (Mark 10:13-16). Jesus knew that *both* little girls and little boys needed the elements of care, love, nurture, teaching, family, and blessings!

Look at who is raising Cain today! Adam and Eve's two sons, Cain and Abel, had a problem. Cain solved it by committing murder, and as the Bible says he became "a vagabond," which means "a waverer or wanderer." A perfect description of many of today's young.

Who really is raising Cain today? The TV is a favored babysitter; computer games waste hours; cell phones, Facebook, Twitter, and text messages consume countless hours; movies, the internet, and more technologies waste up to an average of seven hours per day with our young. Add to that, working families have two or more jobs, further reducing the time to influence their young. According to Journalist Lesley Alderman, dads are now spending an average of 7.8 hours per week on child care. "Moms clock almost double this." (Lesley Alderman, *The Book of Time*s, as quoted in *PEOPLE* magazine, 2/18/2013)

The life cycle for a typical child of working parents or single parents goes something like this: Birth, which is quickly followed by a day-care center (as early as infant-care or by age two or three), followed by kindergarten, then twelve years in a public school, followed possibly by college. By the time a child is twenty-two years old and has completed college, he or she has been imparted knowledge by day care workers, teachers, and professors for sev enteen to twenty years! That doesn't leave a whole lot of time to home and parents.

Imparting instruction and beginning a legacy must begin at home at an early age! Here are some of the specifics and responsibilities as given in the Torah for all of us to follow:

Fix these words of Mine in your hearts and minds; tie them as symbols on your hands and bind them on your foreheads (Deuteronomy 11:18).

Here is where it all begins. This is specifically, intentionally given truth to all parents and all mentors! Begin with yourself. What kind of an example are you living and leaving so that your footprints can be followed by the next generation? No longer can you say to the young, "Do as I say, not as I am doing!" No more excuses!

Influence—everybody talks about it; few really understand it; most parents really want it; but sadly few really achieve it. Parenthood and leadership comes alive with positive influence. Everybody influences someone! Mom and Dad are the most powerful influencer in the lives of little ones! Make sure that you continue your influence until that child is ready to leave home. Who else will counter some of the garbage being poured into their little heads that are full of mush?

The following is a plaque that was given out by a church on Father's Day to all the men who were present. The author is unknown:

Passing the Baton

The Little Chap Who Follows Me
A careful man I want to be,
A little fellow follows me;
I do not dare to go astray
For fear he'll go the self-same way.

I cannot once escape his eyes.
Whate'er he sees me do he tries.
Like me he says he's going to be...
That little chap who follows me.

I must remember as I go
Through summer suns and winter snows,
I am building for the years to be...
That little chap who follows me!

The issue is not whether you influence your kids and family. What we need to settle here and now is *what kind* of an influencer or parent are you? The truth is that you can grow in your parenting skills! Believe that! We start with "position" leadership because you are a parent!

A parent is great, not because of your position power but because of your ability to empower others! "Success without a successor is a failure," so wrote John Maxwell. Let's look at this from another view—parents without a positive legacy are failures. Really, folks, it's time to parent up. We get only one lifetime to make it work and make it right.

So it all begins with us personally. We need to get our

lifestyle and relationships in order—relationships with the Lord and relationships with our spouse. Live the life and do it right because everyone influences someone, especially our kids. It's been said that the best thing a father can do for their kids is to love their mother!

My Influence
My life shall touch a dozen lives
Before this day is done.
Leave countless marks of good or ill,
E'er sets the evening sun.

This, the wish I always wish,
The prayer I always pray:
LORD, may my life help other lives
It touches by the way.
(Author and source is unknown)

If you are still wondering about the meaning to the reference to "tie them as symbols on your hands and bind them on your foreheads" (Deut. 11:118), here is a simple explanation. They are "phylacteries," strips of parchment with four passages of scriptures written on them in the following order: Deuteronomy 11:13-22; 6:4-9; Exodus 13:11-16; 13:1-10. Each strip is rolled up, tied with the white hairs of a cow's tail, and placed in a small box. These are to be the words used during prayer and attached to the forehead between the eyebrows and on the left arm, so as to be near the heart. You can observe this practice in modern Israel, today. For us it would be significant in that we can memorize the Word of God and have it in our heart and mind as we lead our families.

Our second scripture:

Teach them to your children, talking about them when you sit at home and when you walk along the road, when you lie down and when you get up (Deuteronomy 11:19).

These are more specifics on how to impart to your offspring the principles of legacy living. These are more than mere suggestions—they are a command!

"Teach them"—means to begin in infancy and the preschool years. I cannot tell you how important the first five years are in developing a child's personality. The teen years will see the value system of your children being developed, the late teens and early twenties are a development of that person's work ethic. Children learn *values* at home, *knowledge* may come from good schooling, and *habits* are influenced by family, friends, and peers. But all of these developments, including a spiritual foundation, must be started early! You can't begin too early!

The first thing Jewish kids learn is how to pray a foundational creed, "Hear, O Israel: The Lord our God, the Lord is One!" (Deuteronomy 6:4) This prayer is repeated as a part of the morning prayers and evening prayers. Learning how to pray should also be at the heart of our Christianity!

They next learn the eighteen parts of a Jewish liturgy

(it's called *shmonch esre*) in which they are taught how to bless. Blessings are offered such as the following normal prayer over their food, "Blessed are You, O Lord, King of the universe who brings forth bread from the earth." That's for the little ones. Later, when the child is older, this prayer may be expanded to include: "Blessed are You, O Lord, King of the universe who creates the fruit of the vine...who creates various types of fruit...who had created everything."

It begins early, it's line upon line, repetition "when you sit at home." Home activities, simple chores, quiet times, and reading to them, include them in as many ways and times as possible.

"When you walk along the road..." If you currently don't take walks with your kids, now is a good time to start. Although the Bible had no concept about how we will be commuting and delivering our kids to school, play, sports, music lessons, and who else knows where...use this time wisely. When you commute, communicate!

"When you lie down and when you get up..." Every morning and every night, teach, talk, repeat prayers, read to them, read the Bible to them. One of the most important things is to begin the day and end the day with the pronouncement of a blessing. What to say? The best blessing is found in Numbers 6:24-26, "The Lord bless you (insert your child's name) and keep you; the Lord make His face shine upon you and be gracious to you; the Lord turn His face toward you and give you peace." Why is this so important? It carries a vital instruction on how to apply or repeat this blessing, The Lord said to Moses, "Tell Aaron and his sons, 'This is how you are to bless...say to them...'" It's to be a spoken blessing! Say to them! Speak into them! Speak over them! Say it...repeat it daily!

So that we clearly understand and get the picture, this responsibility is a serious assignment given to all of us who are interested in building a lasting legacy. It's a daily habit. (Speaking of habits, if an action is repeated at least twenty-one days in succession, it becomes a habit.) Prayer, Bible reading, respect for elders, sharing meaningful leisure activities, meal time prayers of blessing, toys that are helpful in teaching life concepts, and a whole lot more should become habits. As we can see, training children is a daily responsibility.

Our third scripture:

Write them on the door-frames of your houses and on your gates (Deuteronomy 11:20).

Have you ever heard of the *mezuzah*? When in Israel, take special note of doorways and doorframes and entrances. In the homes of the Torah-observing Jews and in many hotels and businesses you will see this strange object—a rectangular, metal box about four inches in length and maybe a half inch wide by a half inch deep, and it's hollow. They take all kinds of shapes. The mezuzah developed from this scripture and the command to place God's Word on their door-frames and gates of your houses. This command is also found first in Deuteronomy 6:6-9.

How Do We Build Our Legacy?

Inside of these boxes you will find a small scroll, rolled up, written with the words from these two passages listed above that we have just read. On the outside usually there will be written in Hebrew, the Hebrew letter *shin* (sort of like a "w"), which is the twenty-first letter in their alphabet. This represents the first letter in God's name, El Shaddai. The word mezuzah is the Hebrew word for "doorpost." The purpose is always to remind the Hebrews of the blood of the lamb applied to the doorposts and lintels of their dwellings when their exodus out of Egypt took place. It is to remind God to protect those living in the house.

The mezuzah is to be attached to the right side of the door at a slight angle, about shoulder height. It's a custom to kiss the right hand and touch the mezuzah when you enter or when you leave. It is to be a constant reminder that all the people who live in the house are to keep God's Word in all their activities, which take place inside as well as outside the home!

What are you doing to have a constant reminder to all who are a part of your house that God's Word is important and the guide for living in this twenty-first century? How has your home been decorated? Art can be a constant reminder of truth. Use your God-given wisdom as to the actions you will take to make this imparting of God's Word and truth a constant in your life and living.

Perhaps this is the place to remind you that all the knowledge and wisdom and truth you have acquired over your years will do you no good unless these truths are lived out.

Simple Concepts To Impart Truth to the Next Generation:

- Regular church attendance! Teach them this habit while they're young. All of us need the fellowship and teaching and encouragement from a positive community. A good church becomes one of your support systems and reinforces your home habits of right living.

- Build important habits into young lives. Simple acts such as regular brushing and flossing; picking up the messes they make; eating healthy; fun family times and celebrations; multi-generational experiences; making their bed every day; thrift habits; the practice of generosity beginning with God and the tithe; respecting others; helping others with their life needs.

- Begin and end the day with a blessing! Regularly read the Bible with them and to them. Lead them in prayers of blessing.

- Provide good literature! We practiced this by selecting the books to read and gave them a reward when completed. Then a report was written or the concepts were discussed around the dinner table.

- Always allow them to see your example of being a giver and not a taker. For example, take them with you as you

How Do We Build Our Legacy?

help a neighbor or as you volunteer in your church or hospital or nursing home.

- After they have fallen to sleep, after you have blessed them and tucked them into bed, speak into their subconscious mind. Tell them of your love; tell them of God's love; tell them of their worth. (This was a practice we initiated after our third son was brain-damaged in an accident. We learned more about the brain than we wanted because as a family, we were the re-hab for Kent. Speaking into the subconscious mind while the child sleeps was one of the recommended ways by his medical team for his future re-programming.)

- Include them in your work projects. Give them the opportunity to understand how this life works and functions. Build something together. Bake something together. Teach them how to work with hands and brains.

- Set strict limits on television watching, cell phone usage, i-pad games. In fact, it might be helpful to totally restrict some of these time wasters. Demonstrate how time is so valuable and how to fill their time with meaningful habits.

- Help them nurture a thirst for learning. Create in them a love for reading and a love for new discoveries.

Are you catching the implications of *imparting before you are departing* to the next generation. From birth to about five is the very best life-time opportunity you will have that is God given to be the parent or grandparent to best equip your next generations for a meaningful lifestyle that works in the twenty-first century.

TAKE AWAY TRUTH: We do not have to re-invent the concepts of good parenting that impart lifetime truths for the next generation. You cannot count on anybody else to replace your responsibilities. You have only one lifetime to invest in others. God has the best plan for multi-generational concepts. Remember, God is always a long term planner and wants to extend your influence to the next four generations and on to a thousand generations! Your influence never ends. It only stops when you have departed after you have imparted!

TEN

Passing the Family Blessing to the Next Generation

God created man (mankind) in His own image, in the image of God He created them (him); male and female He created them. God blessed them! God saw all that he had made, and it was very good! (Genesis 1:27-28, 31)

How would you like to be supernaturally blessed in your future, your finances, your health, your relationships, and your emotions? As a result you will be filled with peace and experience a joy that is unspeakable, have a victory over the flesh and the devil, and even change the dynamics in your family.

One of the major secrets is found and is to be discovered in this thing called The Blessing! This is one of those biblical mysteries or secrets that has largely been lost to the church for about two thousand years. However, we have seen how the Jewish people have been practicing in their exceptional lifestyle (at least the Torah believing and practicing Jews) from Abraham's time down to the present. We need to really re-discover this truth and put it into practice so as to bless the next generations!

We have talked about the blessing and implied the power of the blessing in this book to this point...however, we have not defined it nor explained how that we, today, in the twenty-first century can experience the blessing. Or we have shied away from practicing it because it has been so muchly abused by others, or mis-used by too many television evangelists. Let's not throw out the baby with the bath water. It's a powerful truth that we need in today's world and if we are to influence the next generation, we need the blessing of God.

First of all, please understand that a biblical blessing is not a blessing until it is a spoken blessing. Every blessing in the Bible was spoken before it was written. Here's how it's to be done according to the Lord: The Lord said to Moses, "Tell Aaron and his sons, this is how you are to bless... say to them...The Lord bless you..." (Numbers 6:22-27) How to bless? Say to them, the people or person you are blessing!

Also note that it is always God's will to bless you and yours! This is not because you or I or they are such wonderful and deserving folk...It's because God is a God of love, a God of mercy, a God of grace, and a God of the blessing! God blesses because He has chosen to be the God of blessing!

So how can we define The Blessing? Simply, a blessing is the favor of God in your life and living. A blessing is the impartation of the supernatural power of God into another human life as spoken by a delegated authority of God!

Words have life and words have meaning, and they have power to bless and change others, especially when spoken by you as a spiritual authority. So who are the delegated or designated authorities of God?

> *But YOU are a chosen people, YOU (implied) are a royal priesthood, YOU are a holy nation, YOU are a people belonging to God, that YOU may declare the praises of Him who called YOU out of darkness into His wonderful light. Once YOU were not a people, but now YOU are the people of God; once YOU had not received mercy, but now YOU have received mercy* (I Peter 2:9-10, emphasis added).

Why? So that you can pass this wonderful relationship and blessing to the next generation! We have replaced the Old Testament regimen of who were the blessors. Today it's our responsibility because we have become the royal priesthood! There is another admonishment that must not be overlooked,

> *Live such good lives among the pagans that, though they accuse you of doing wrong, they may see your good deeds and glorify God* (vs. 12).

The pagans and heathens of this world need to see these truths lived out. It's not a politically correct world that must be the major influencer in the living of our children. It's you and I who, in spite of being accused of doing it wrong, need to do it right beginning with today!

There are at least five applications or definitions or uses of the blessing:

1. To make someone or something complete, whole or holy by spoken words;
2. To wish a person or situation well;
3. To make prosperous the body, mind, and soul;
4. To invoke or ask for divine favor or the favor of others;
5. To make a person happy or glad or joyful!

According to Gary Smalley and John Trent (*The Blessing*, Nelson House, Nashville, TN, 1986), there are five basic parts to a blessing: A meaningful touch; a spoken message; attaching high value to the one being blessed; picturing a special future for the one being blessed; and an active commitment to fulfill the blessing. It can be restated like this, "A blessing begins with a meaningful touch. It continues with a spoken message of high value, a message that pictures a special future for the individual being blessed, and one that is based on an active commitment to see the blessing come to pass in that person's life."

The following are the most common Jewish blessings pronounced, prayed over and spoken daily and particularly on the Sabbath as part of their weekly celebration. For boys: "May God make you as Ephraim and Manasseh!" For girls: "May God make you as Sarah, Leah, Rebekah, and Rachel." See how simple—short and to the point. You need not make your daily blessings new or lengthy, but they should be repetitive.

A brief study of The Blessing will give you many clues as to what and to whom and how to bless!

The FIRST BLESSING was pronounced by God after He had created the critters, all the living things, animals, God blessed them and said, "Be fruitful and increase in number..." (Genesis 1:20-24).

The SECOND BLESSING was pronounced by God on the sixth day when "God created man in His own image, in the image of God He created...male and female He created them. God blessed them and said to them..." (Genesis 1:26-28)

The THIRD blessing followed the creation of the seventh day, "And God blessed the seventh day and made it holy..." (Genesis 2:2-3).

The FOURTH appearance followed the flood and ushered in a whole new beginning, "Then God blessed Noah and his family(sons), saying to them..." (Genesis 9:1).

Now we move on to the call of Abram when God laid the foundation for a new nation through whom the whole world would be blessed, "I will make YOU into a great nation and I will bless you..." (Genesis 12:1-3). This was blessing number FIVE and a far reaching blessing.

The SIXTH blessing was the first recorded by a human who blessed another, "Then Melchizedek king of Salem (Jerusalem) brought out bread and wine. He was the priest of God Most High and he blessed Abraham, saying..." (Genesis 14:18-20).

The SEVENTH blessing is unique in that an angel of the

Lord added, "I will increase your descendants that they will be too numerous to count" (Genesis 16:9-11). This blessing was given to Hagar in her misery and to her son Ishmael, another blessing that is currently in force in today's world for good or bad.

The EIGHT and NINTH blessings were spoken by God to Sarah and promised a son (Genesis 17:15-21) and established that the covenant of blessing is on to the next generation, Isaac.

The TENTH was a promise of blessing that was re-stated to Abraham after it had earlier been given to Hagar (Genesis 21:12-13). Next came the blessing following the obedience of Abraham as he was willing to sacrifice his son, Isaac, (Genesis 22:17-18).

The ELEVENTH mention of a blessing is recorded of siblings blessing their sister as she leaves her family home to begin a new life as the wife of Isaac, (Genesis 59-60). The next blessing to consider is the blessing of God, fulfilling the early blessing given to Abraham, now God says it is to continue to the next generation, "After Abraham's death, God blessed his son, Isaac" (Genesis 25:11). That blessing was further expanded to cover a difficult and devastating time in the life of Isaac when he faced a famine, "Stay in the land for a while and I will be with you and will bless you" (Genesis 26:2-6). The benefit was that he planted and harvested a 100 times increase in the middle of a famine!

Passing the Family Blessing to the Next Generation

Then there are a listing of numerous blessings that were spoken from one generation to the next: Isaac blessed Jacob and Esau; Jacob blessed his grandsons and twelve sons; Jacob blessed Joseph; Joseph blessed the household of Potiphar as well as all of Egypt; and Moses blessed Israel and more. There are lots of practical lesson on the blessing to be learned from these that blessed animals, new beginnings, the first family, families, siblings, grandchildren, crops, a nation, the world... absolutely incredible! And perhaps, most importantly, we can bless our families and others and situations and circumstances!

But the most important blessing that we can take part in is the privilege to bless the Lord God almighty, the King of all kings and the Lord of all lords! We need to learn how to bless instead of whining, complaining, griping, and criticizing! King David found this secret in learning how to "Bless the Lord, oh my soul and all that is within me! Bless His holy name!"

The Blessing, for sure, is to be shared with the next generation. When passing a blessing, you may be thinking, "What can I say or should say when pronouncing a blessing on others?" I'm glad you asked. The following are at least thirty (30) things you can say based on the biblical patterns: God bless you with ability!

1. God bless you with abundance!
2. God bless you with clear directions in your life!
3. God bless you with angelic protection!

4. God bless you with the assurance of His love, grace, mercy, and love!

5. God bless you with a controlled and disciplined lifestyle!

6. God bless you with courage!

7. God bless you with creativity!

8. God bless you with spiritual perception of God's truth!

9. God bless you with ever increasing faith!

10. God bless you with His favor and the favor of mankind!

11. God bless you with good health, divine health and healing!

12. God bless you with a good spouse!

13. God bless you with helping hands in order to be able to help

14. God bless you with joy and happiness!

15. God bless you with a satisfying life fulfillment!

16. God bless you with contentment!

17. God bless you with hope and a good outlook on life!

18. God bless you with a listening ear and empathy for others!

19. God bless you with contentment!

20. God bless you with an obedient heart to the Holy Spirit of God!

21. God bless you with pleasant speech!

22. God bless you with His peace that is beyond understanding!

23. God bless you with a pleasing personality and sound character!

24. God bless you with promotion!

25. God bless you with his divine protection!

26. God bless you with provision, safety and strength for every day!

27. God bless you with His success!

28. God bless you with trust and godly wisdom!

29. God bless you with goodness and mercy that will follow you all the days of your long life, so that together we may dwell in the house of the Lord forever!

The Jewish people have employed these concepts of the blessing, as I have previously noted, from Abraham's day down to our day. Each Sabbath, as part of their celebration, these mothers and fathers bless their children in the name of the God of Abraham, Isaac and Jacob. When they take these kids to the synagogue, as a part of the worship, time in the service is given to the children when the Rabbi and Elders call the children forward and bless them.

When the girls reach age twelve and the boys reach age thirteen, there is a very special celebration called "bat" mitzvah for girls and a "bar" mitzvah for boys. (The age difference is because girls mature quicker than boys.) This is a celebration of coming of age when they are blessed by parents, grandparents and the Rabbi. What are they saying? Why are they doing this? They are literally shaping the destiny and future of their children who are considered to be adults with adult responsibilities. It's a coming of age public ceremony and done in a real happy, party celebration complete with food, music, gifts, toasts, prayers, blessings, and fun!

The basis for this goes all the way back to Abraham and the blessing he passed on to Isaac. This was re-affirmed in the life of Jesus Christ. His miraculous birth was followed with circumcision on the eighth day when he was blessed and his parents were blessed by Simeon the priest and Anna the prophetess. When Jesus was age 12, according to Luke 2:22, 28-34, he appeared in the Temple and spoke with the religious leaders. Now any Jewish Rabbi will tell you that in reality, Jesus was thirteen because Jews celebrate birthdays at conception not at birth so Christ was thirteen, and this is considered to have been his bar mitzvah.

One other important thing may also take place at these celebrations. I was fascinated as I listened to a Rabbi explain that at this time a "minion" is created for each child. A minion is a group of ten adults who are at least thirty years of age and become the mentors for this child until he or she reaches the age of thirty. The parents take on a different role as each life decision is presented before this group who will guide the decision making process.

They are taught logic and Jewish concepts of business, are given pointers on where to continue their education, whom they are to marry, and much more!

Think of how our society and culture could be changed with this kind of a reinforcement on how to live. Does it work? Let me share one thought—in America, we have been told that about 50% of first time marriages will end in divorce; 73% of second time marriages will too. Of the Torah practicing Israelites, first time marriages that end in divorce are between 5% to 6%! There are other factors, sure, but here's what I believe is a major factor in making the right kind of life choices! It's constant blessings and more blessings piled upon blessings! No wonder they are and have become a very unique and blessed people as God promised them. As a group, they have not yet accepted Jesus Christ as their Messiah, but they are practicing the Old Testament life principles. Think of what can happen in your family combining the biblical teachings with a personal relationship with the Messiah. Think of the wonderful, exciting possibilities for your future and generation building!

How We as a Family Pass the Blessing

These truths are so exciting...however, they did not really become a part of our family until the Christmas of 1997. I developed a health condition called chronic atrophic largnytis. (My voice box dried up—there was no more lubrication—plus it was a nearly pre-cancerous throat condition.) I lost my voice and my ability to speak in public. I had to resign as a senior pastor—a pastor without a voice is a pastor without a church. As the final sermon series to my wonderful congregation, I wanted to leave them something memorable. I was directed to The Blessing and prepared and preached a four-part series. There was a final farewell celebration, and as of October 1, I was no longer a senior pastor. It was the most dramatic and soul-wrenching life change I had ever faced. What would I do now? (To answer your question—yes, a healing has taken place, and I am now able to do public speaking and writing. This is a quick background so you can understand where I am coming from with The Blessing!)

After my retirement, the Holy Spirit kept bouncing these concepts through Donna (my wife) and I. We began thinking of how best to bring to life the blessing in our family. Why allow the Jews to have all the fun? Up to this point, we had practiced living in The Blessing and often spoke blessings over our own kids. The thought came alive as we brainstormed. Why not have a Christian bar mitzvah and bat mitzvah for our grandchildren when they reached ages twelve for girls or thirteen for boys?

We decided that it would become a part of our family celebration at Christmas because this was usually the only time all of us gathered together. (Our family is scattered from South Dakota to Tennessee and to Arkansas, and we live in Missouri.) That Christmas of 1997 would be our first special passing of The Blessing. We alerted our own adult children to come prepared with a special written blessing to be spoken over Christopher, our oldest grandson who had turned thirteen in 1997.

Following the giving of gifts and the Christmas feast, we all gathered in the living room. There were seventeen of us, adults and kids, along with three dogs. In the middle of our circle was a "blessing" chair. Christopher, eyes wide open, just not knowing what was about to take place, sat in the chair. I took the time to read some important scriptures in regards to the blessing—Genesis 12:1-4 and Numbers 6:22-27—and explained to the other seven grandkids what this was all about.

Grandma Donna began with the first blessing. She laid a hand on Chris and read her prayerfully prepared blessing. Before she had finished, the emotion of the moment overtook our family—there was not a dry eye among us. The next blessing was read by his youngest aunt, Cheriee, then her husband; this continued with Uncle Kent; Aunt Becky and Uncle Marc; then his own parents, Kirk and Jennifer; and the final blessing was given by me, Grandpa Bob. Then a specific prayer for Chris, and his parents presented him with a Bible by which to remember this day. Then his mother, Jennifer, gathered up all the written blessings and placed them into a "blessing" book—a memory and a hard copy!

What makes this so powerful? When the instructions had been given to Moses by God, "This is how you are to bless...say to them..." The kicker in this passing the blessing is found in the last verse: "So they will put my name on the Israelites, and I will bless them!" (Numbers

6:22-27). In other words, by the spoken word, you can mark others for God. You can put something into their personhood that marks them and their future for God. We chose this kind of a celebration, a time to be marked forever into young psyches, something indelible that cannot be erased. It is an event just like the passing of the blessing to Jacob and Esau.

Well, let's continue. The next Christmas it was Kristie's turn to be blessed. All the adults had prepared her blessing, and Christopher also had a prepared blessing to share with his cousin! He was now considered an adult with adult responsibilities. And so it went on to Sarah, Cody, Casey, and Jonathan. Kristie blessed her sister Sarah and brother Jonathan. Christopher blessed his brother Cody and sister Casey. What an unforgettable time as each of these grandchildren eagerly anticipated their blessing.

If you know our family, there were two others yet to be blessed, Benjamin and Maxwell, but there was a break because of their ages. Therefore, the next Christmas we blessed Marc, our oldest son, and his wife, Becky. Again all the blessed grandkids now blessed their parents. What an adventure in family relationships! The next year it was Kirk and Jennifer, then Cheriee and her spouse, and finally Kent who is single and remains at home.

One other element was introduced when I, Grandpa, prepared and pronounced a family blessing along with the written copies to be attached on a refrigerator or framed for everybody. These became part of the blessing books.

One day I got a call from Becky, our oldest daughter-in-law. "Dad, I have to tell you what happened. Today Kristie came home from school and slammed her way through the front door, and I immediately knew something bad had happened in her day. She stomped her way down the hall to her room and slammed the door! All was quiet. I gave her about fifteen minutes to cool down. Then I went to her door and gently knocked. She knew it was me, she said, 'Okay Mom, come in.' As I entered her bedroom she was sitting cross-legged on her bed with her Blessing Book opened. Tears were coursing down her cheeks as she read where she was in the Strand family, how blessed she was, and how important she was to the Lord." (Make sure the blessings you share can be remembered and re-read over and over again!) Mark them with the name of God.

And, oh yes, we haven't forgotten Benjamin and Maxwell. We have also had two step-grandchildren added to our family who also will be blessed.

There are churches where I have been privileged to make the blessing presentation who are also celebrating the blessing for each thirteen-year-old son or daughter. You can invite family, neighbors, and friends to your special blessing presentation for your children.

Not only can you share a special blessing at becoming of age, don't overlook other special times to bless: graduations, weddings, anniversaries, promotions at work, completions of projects, along with many more.

Let's put a wrap on this chapter by way of perspective. Jack Hayford said: "Of all the tools God gave you to raise a child, the most powerful is your tongue! Use it for good!"

The power to speak blessings is shown early in the Bible. God spoke blessings on His creations; Noah blessed Shem and Japheth; Abraham blessed Isaac; Melchizedek blessed Abraham. There's a powerful principle here: God has given all of us the privilege and power to speak blessings upon others, especially on our children. This blessing is to advance a positive life that honors God and advances good health, growth, a future, joy, and self-confidence.

The imparting of a blessing can be reflected in our everyday activities, the simple things. A word in season, how good it is in a child's life! Approval and love and value and being cared for are important to every child. It's a pattern of blessing that God, who is our ultimate Father, has shown His love for us. Consider the following:

- A warm embrace, a hug, an arm around a shoulder is priceless, especially when a child has been disappointed or is experiencing fear or doubt. *(read Deuteronomy 33:27; Isaiah 40:28-31, 41:10)*

- A pat on the back, encouragement at critical moments when little ones need a helping hand. *(read Psalm 139:5-6, 14-15)*

- How about a whisper which conveys a quiet, "you can do it" or passing along a secret plan or instructions. *(read Isaiah 30:19-21, vs. 21 is the key)*

- Put them to bed, making sure they know they are loved and protected even in the dark of night. *(read Psalm 127:2-5)*

- Show affection, a kiss on the cheek, bounce them on your knee, hold them tightly, give tender love and soft caresses. *(read Psalm 103:13-41, 17-18)*

If you happen to go back in history and read the biographies of people born 100 to 150 years ago or so, you will note some things of interest. First, many more families suffered the loss of a child, making a devastating impact on their lives. Second, many more children grew up in cold and emotionally distant homes, where a father barely knew their kids and found it nearly impossible to express love for them. Third, parents as well as the people who studied them were also emotionally diffident.

In 1938 Harvard University began a study that was to track students during their lifetime. The plan was to measure, test, and interview them at five year intervals to see how their lives developed.

Early on, the researchers didn't pay much attention to men's relationships. Instead they paid a lot of attention to the men's physiognomy, masculine body types, and genetics.

But as this study progressed, the power of relationships became very clear. They found that the men who grew up in homes with warm, loving parents, were much more likely to become leaders, as demonstrated in WWII by the fact that these men became first lieutenants, captains, majors, and colonels. But the men who grew up in cold, barren, loveless homes ended up as privates.

George Vaillant, the study director sums it up in *Triumphs of Experience,* a summary of this research, said: "What goes right is more important than what goes wrong!" The positive effect of at least one loving relative, parent, mentor, or friend can overwhelm the negative effects of the bad things that happen! The men who could be affectionate, loving toward people, combined with persistence, discipline, order, and dependability, had very enjoyable lives!

However, a childhood does not totally determine a life. The beauty of the study is that, as Vaillant emphasizes, the really big finding is that you *can* teach an old dog new tricks! He found that the men who survived to old age kept changing for the better even while in their 70s, 80s, and even into their 90s. There is hope for all of us!

Physical acts of encouragement are wonderful, but I remind you again that the most affirming blessings will come in your words. We are back where we started with The Blessing—a blessing begins with a meaningful touch, it continues with a spoken message of high value, a message that pictures a special future or the child or individual being blessed and one that is based on an active commitment that you will do all you can to see the blessing come to pass in this life! It is humbling to think that God has given us an unbelievably powerful tool and the responsibility to go along with it, that when spoken it is possible to cause good things to happen! YOU can do it!

TAKE AWAY TRUTH: You too like Abraham, Isaac, Jacob, Melchizedek, Moses, the sons of Levi, and all of you who are a part of God's royal priesthood can pass the blessing! Use your God-given creativity as to how and when it can be done and should be done. Don't allow the busyness of life cause you to neglect these once-in-lifetime opportunities to bless the next generation pass you by!

NOTE: Should you desire to explore this concept much more in depth, please get a copy of *The B Word* and *Breaking Generational Curses* published by Evergreen Press, Mobile, Alabama (see info at front of book), on the Internet, or at your local bookstore. If they don't have it, they can order one for you.

ELEVEN

Live To Be One Hundred and Twenty

...for he (mankind) is mortal: his (or her) days will be a hundred and twenty years! (Genesis 6:3)

This edict was God's promise for all of us and His intention that we should have a full healthy life until 120! Or there is another scripture:

We finish our years with a moan. The length of our days is seventy years or eighty, if we have the strength! (Psalm 90:10)

This verse is part of a pessimistic prayer or complaint to God by Moses. But then consider that...

Moses was a hundred and twenty years old when he died, yet his eyes were not weak nor his strength gone! (Deuteronomy 34:7)

And don't overlook the example of Caleb who said...

So here I am...85 years old! I am still as strong today as the day Moses sent me out; I'm just as vigorous to go to battle now as I was then. Now give me this (mountain) hill country that the Lord promised me that day! (Joshua 14:10-11)

Here is a testimonial to the good health that was part of God's plan...

He brought them forth also with silver and gold; and there was not one feeble person among their tribes! (Psalm 105:37, KJV)

What am I doing including a chapter on living a long life in a book about building a four generation legacy? How can you be the mentor, the parent, grandparent or great-grandparent that God has intended you to be if you spend your life, your energy, and resources struggling with disease, poor health, bad habits, poor nutrition, and no exercise? Wouldn't it be a fabulous life bonus to be able to live to 120 so you can enjoy your fourth generation and be able and vigorous enough to keep up with the younger generations? Think of the joy of watching and nurturing the foundations you have laid, the mentoring you have done, the sacrifices on behalf of future generations that could be fulfilled in your life time! God has planned that we should live in maximum health so that we can carry out His purposes in our life style!

Dr. Don Colbert, M.D. wrote: "I believe the Word of God promises Christians 120 years of life (see Genesis 6:3). Yet, instead of living out this promise, most believers accept growing old as a natural process." Living to 120 is not a myth—it is a reality that you can help make come to pass in your life!

Poor health is mostly a matter of choice. Bad choices make us sick while good choices can get us back to health and help us stay healthy. According to Dr. Colbert, who often speaks about studies on centenarians,

> These studies have looked at the traits that enable them to live so long. None of them are smokers, alcoholics or drug addicts. Very few are obese, and while they aren't vegetarians, veggies and fruits are a significant part of their diets. They remain active both physically and mentally. (Don Colbert, *Seven Keys for Living to 120*, CHARISMA, January 2013, p. 38)

Jose Maria Roa lived to 137 and remained in perfect health for his lifetime. He lived in the mountains of the Andes in Ecuador. He worked every day on his small farm and fathered his last child at 107! He was part of a study by Morton Walker, D.P.M., whose book, *Secrets of Long Life*, was based on the natives of the Vilcambamba Valley in Ecuador. Walker concluded:

> As I studied Jose...and people like him...I began to understand the potential that all humans have to be healthy. In America today, we are usually told...and believe...that illnesses like cancer, arthritis, dementia, osteoporosis, diabetes and heart disease are "diseases of aging," but these chronic conditions are not the inevitable result of growing older. Rather, they are the inevitable result of living lifestyles that cannot support human health!

According to the World Health Organization (WHO), the United States ranks thirty-seventh in overall health quality. "It should serve as a wake-up call for all

Americans when a third-world country like Oman spends only $334 per person per year on health and ranks eighth in the world."

An editorial by Joseph Scherger, M.D. in *Hippocrates*, said that "Lifestyle factors now loom as the leading cause of premature death." Compared to studies of such people groups as the Vilcambambans in Ecuador, the Hunzas in northern Pakistan, and the Cuenca Indians in Ecuador, the average American is not doing well at all. We are compromising our health with nutritionally deficient diets, environmental toxins, sedentary lifestyles, chronic stress, bad habits along with the lack of positive emotions or meaningful relationships along with the damaging outcomes of symptom management by modern, conventional medicine. We are plagued with two causes of disease: deficiency and toxicity!

Enough background, so what can we do about our health problems? How is it possible to live to be 120 and still enjoy good health? (Please understand, I am not a medically trained person. However, as a writer and researcher who is an avid reader, I want to share with you some quick, brief concepts, a condensing of a lot of consensus by many experts in the health fields. Also, you need to know that I had the privilege to serve on the Boards of Administration for two different hospital systems, one in Missouri and the other in Colorado. At the end of this chapter, you will find a listing of recommended books from which I have gleaned valuable information.)

Keys for Living to 120

ATTITUDE

This mental, spiritual and psychological key may turn out to be the most important key of all! Here and now, it is time to make the most important decision—that you will do whatever it takes to reach your goal of living in health to 120 years! Make the commitment and set this goal! Your thoughts, emotions, motivations, habits, and actions all affect your health! These thoughts of yours can trigger a whole bunch of reactions that will enhance or damage your health.

What you allow to enter your mind on a daily basis is critical! What we think and what we feel play a major role in our health! Memorize the following:

> *Finally, brothers and sisters, whatever is true, whatever is noble, whatever is right, whatever is pure, whatever is lovely, whatever is admirable...if anything is excellent or praise-worthy...think about such things...put it into practice! And the God of peace* [the God of divine health] *will be with you!* (Philippians 4:8-9)

Let's do an immediate check-up from the neck up! Are you thinking, "This is an impossible goal and I'm not up to it"? It might be a tough and long, steep mountain to climb, so here's your motivation for the task ahead: "I can do everything through him who gives me strength!" If Paul the Apostle could do this with all his problems, not the least of which was to be confined in a dungeon with a death sentence hanging over him, you too can also make it happen because there is a promise attached to your decision: "And my God will meet all your needs according to his glorious riches in Christ Jesus" (Philippians 4:13, 19).

PHYSICAL

Most Americans aren't getting adequate exercise or sleep or sunlight (necessary for Vitamin D). Experts tell us that we all need at least two to three hours per week of exercise, even moderate exercise. The best way to begin is with 15 to 30 minute walks, six days a week. Another excellent way to get your exercise is to get a "rebounder"—a mini trampoline and bounce daily no matter how bad the weather is outside. James White, M.D., of the University of California, San Diego, says that "rebounding exercise is the closest thing to the 'Fountain of Youth' that science has discovered." It's because you are moving and stretching every cell. It helps to supply essential nutrients and eliminates toxic waste products, and your entire body—organs, bones, connective tissue and skin—becomes stronger, more flexible, and healthier.

You are never too old to exercise! Moses, at 120 years of age, climbed a 3,300 foot mountain that many today give up on because it's too tough to climb. Instead they opt for a helicopter ride to the top! "Then Moses climbed Mount Nebo from the plains of Moab to the top of Pisgah, across from Jericho" (Deuternomy 34:1).

And don't forget to make sure you are getting adequate rest! All of us need seven to eight hours of sleep every night. "Any less than this and you're increasing your risk of heart disease, high blood pressure, stroke, diabetes and other diseases. Lack of sleep also ages your skin and increases your chances of gaining weight," according to Don Colbert, M.D.

NUTRITION

What is America's leading cause of disease? "Malnutrition!" according to biochemist and MIT graduate, Raymond Francis, M.Sc. When thinking about malnutrition, pictures of starving children come to mind who live in a third-world country. The typical American diet, which the majority of us eat, does not supply what our bodies need of sufficient nutrition. Why are we having such a problem in eating the right things, the good things, foods that provide us with the necessary things that make for optimum health?

Let's consider one thing: wheat! It almost sounds sacrilegious to portray wheat as a bad guy. Since biblical times, bread and wheat were used as wholesome nourishment and symbolized being "the bread of life." The bread that was broken at the Lord's Last Supper and at the table of your grandparents was a different substance than what we can buy at the supermarket or bakery. Why? Dr. William Davis, M.D., in his book, *Wheat Belly,* makes the claims that today's wheat is:

> ...commercially farmed and has been modified to make it more resistant to insects, fungi and other profit

draining occurrences. Wheat, being the chief profit crop for much of the world has undergone more modification than any other substance. It has been cross-bred and hybridized.

In the simplest terms, the so-called "healthy complex carbs" of modern wheat are worse for blood sugar levels than almost any other type of sugar or carbohydrate. For a real-world example...consuming two slices of whole wheat bread is the same, in terms of increased blood sugar, as drinking a can of sugary soda.

That's one example of store-bought and processed foods. Anything with a label on it has been hybridized and cross-bred and had the good stuff taken out by technology in order to make it easier to use or more profitable. Eat things without labels on them such as asparagus, oranges, apples, carrots, and cucumbers. Eat more fresh and raw foods and load up on veggies. Yes, have a steak once in a while too!

Have you considered the experience of Daniel lately? When Nebuchadnezzar king of Babylon wanted select young men from the conquered city of Jerusalem to enter the king's service, he directed that they eat from the king's table. In response, Daniel said:

> *"Please test your servants for ten days: Give us nothing but vegetables to eat and water to drink. Then compare our appearance with that of the young men who eat the royal food, and treat your servants in accordance with what you see.." So he agreed to this and tested them for ten days. At the*

> end of ten days they looked healthier and better nourished than any of the young men who ate the royal food. So the guard took away their choice food and the wine they were to drink and gave them vegetables instead! To these four young men God gave knowledge and understanding of all kinds (Daniel 1:11-17).

Bio-chemist Raymond Francis writes, "Almost all disease can be prevented or reversed. As a result, health is a choice and no one has to be sick." He goes on to tell us there are not thousands of diseases, but only one disease: malfunctioning cells. If the cells that make up your body are healthy, then you are healthy. Your cells are healthy and balanced when they have proper nutrition and are protected from toxins. Simple as that—healthy cells equals a healthy body.

SPIRITUAL AND EMOTIONAL

Are you aware that in the Bible, the word "rejoice" appears 248 times? The words "joy, joyfulness, and joyfully" can be found more than 200 times! And the word "laugh" has been penned 40 times in the Bible! Here's a "laugh prescription" written by Dr. William Fry, a psychiatrist at the Stanford University Medical School:

> Laugh 100 times a day and you may feel like an idiot, but you'll be in great shape! In fact, you'll have given your heart the same workout you'd get if you pedaled on a stationary bike for 15 minutes. Over time, chuckling this much also lowers blood pressure and heart rate,

reduces pain, strengthens the immune system and cuts down on stress-creating hormones. The biggest problem is finding that many things to laugh about!

To be joyful is an attitude, a mind-set, a decision, and a discipline! "Laughter is joy flowing, happiness showing, countenance showing kind of an attitude!" so wrote Charles R. Swindoll.

How would you like to add seven more years to your life? Dr. Harold G. Koenig of Duke University wrote:

> Studies have shown prayer can prevent people from getting sick and if and when they do get sick, prayer can help them get better faster. An exhaustive analysis of more than 1,500 reputable medical studies indicates people who are more religious and pray more have better mental and physical health. And out of 125 studies that looked at the link between health and regular worship, 85% showed regular church-goers live longer!

Tom Knox, researcher and writer, who was at one-time an atheist, became a regular worshiper after doing in-depth study of the medical benefits of faith wrote:

> What I have discovered astonished me! Over the past 30 years a growing body of scientific work shows religious belief is medically, socially and psychologically beneficial. Religious attendance is associated with adult mortality in a graded fashion. There is a seven year difference in the life expectancy between those who never attend church and those who attend weekly!

That's not all, "Population Researchers" at the University of Texas discovered "the more often you go to church, the longer you live!" *The United States Journal of Gerontology* revealed that "atheists, in a study of 4,000 older adults, had a significantly increased chance of dying six to seven years sooner than the faithful! Real religious people live longer than atheists!"

Surely goodness and love will follow me all the days of my life, and I will dwell in the house of the Lord forever (Psalm 23:6).

Better is one day in your courts than a thousand elsewhere; I would rather be a doorkeeper in the house of my God than dwell in the tents of the wicked. For the Lord is a sun and shield; the Lord bestows favor and honor; no good thing does He withhold from those whose walk is blameless. O Lord Almighty, blessed is the man (or woman or family) who trusts in you (Psalm 84:10-12).

I rejoiced with those who said to me, "Let us go to the house of the Lord" (Psalm 122:1).

Unless the Lord builds the house (family), its builders labor in vain. Unless the Lord watches over the city, the watchmen stand guard in vain...for He grants sleep to those He loves. Sons and daughters are a heritage from the Lord, children a reward from Him (Psalm 127:1-3).

Blessed are all who fear the Lord, who walk in His ways. You will eat the fruit of your labor; blessings and prosperity will be yours (Psalm 128:1-2).

FASTING

Early in our married life, Donna and I had a family doctor who encouraged his patients to practice regular fasting as a part of his care for them. His practice was to fast one day per week, usually on Fridays because this was his busiest day. I asked him why.

He replied, "I do this on a regular basis to rid my body of toxins, to cleanse it, to give the digestive tract a rest, to improve my sleep, to keep my weight in check, for the pure discipline of it, and don't forget the spiritual value of fasting."

When Jesus was teaching His disciples basic principles of godly living in Matthew 6:16, He addressed fasting like this, "*When* you fast..." not "*If* you fast!" These words of His imply that fasting should be a regular practice in the lifestyles of all of His followers. Despite the fact that fasting is taught often in the Bible, too many Christians have not yet embraced this powerful spiritual, healthful, and mental discipline. (Check with your family doctor before you do a major fast.)

Briefly, when you fast, you deny yourself of food or certain foods for a specified period of time. When you commit to a fast, it's like saying, "Lord, nothing is more important to me than you!" There are basically three different types of fasts:

Absolute: no food or water—but this is not recommended for most of us. *Liquid*: Water only or fruit and vegetable juices and/or a combination of both. *Partial*:

When eating certain food groups and restricting others as Daniel and the three Hebrew children did.

Anyone who has fasted one meal or food for a day, three days, ten days, or even forty days would probably agree that it might be difficult. They would also agree that the sacrifices are well worth the rewards! Just try it...you might like it!

There is an incredible abundance of research, concepts, diets, teachings, CDs, DVDs, and resources beyond the brief listings above. Please take note and arm yourself, learn how to listen to your own doctor that lives in your mind, body, and soul. With what is happening today within our government and "The Patient Protection and Affordable Care Act" (Obamacare) and other problems with health care, you need to take charge of your own health! Begin listening to the doctor within you and take your own health as your responsibility. Nobody cares about your well-being like you!

The church at large and your family should be concerned about health care. Why? The simple answer is because Jesus was. In America, we have believed that no matter what we do with our bodies, doctors can use medicine and technology to fix them when they break down. Unfortunately conventional medical treatment can't cure anything, it only treats the symptoms and is not always that good at it!

Rev. Scott Morris, M.D., who is a Methodist minister

and family physician who is the founder of the Church Health Center in Memphis, Tennessee says:

> Churches have the potential to be power-houses of life-giving community by advocating for prevention, and teaching people how to care for both their bodies and their spirits, and how to live healthy lifestyles. Revitalization of the church will not come from bad Christian rock music, but it may indeed come from creative, active, health ministries all over the country.

I would be remiss if I didn't include the following information that will not make your day. In fact, this may be a shock to your system, your thinking, your eating habits, and your future. There is a huge body of researchers who have come to the consensus about the four worst food choices, which comprise the bulk of the average American diet and are disastrous to your health and are to be avoided at all costs! They are:

1. SUGAR

Sugar wreaks havoc on your system! If you make only one change in your diet, let it be to eliminate or at least reduce your intake of sugar by 75%! Harvey Diamond, in his book, *Fit for Life: A New Beginning* calls refined sugar "a deadly, virulent poison."

Did you know that the average American eats a whopping 160 pounds or more of sugar a year! The problem is that sugar is found in almost all processed foods; it's almost impossible to avoid so learn how to read labels! Too many kids receive almost half of their calories from sugar. Biochemist Raymond Francis, M.Sc. writes: "Sugar is an anti-nutrient...eating sugar drains nutrients from your body. Sugar causes and contributes to enormous problems such as diabetes, tooth decay, heart disease, osteoporosis and immune dysfunction. Eating sugar is death by installment!"

Again...if you make only one change in your diet, eliminate or reduce your sugar intake! Now, is that too bad? Hold on, it just gets worse and it takes more than a spoonful of sugar to let the medicine go down!

2. WHEAT AND WHITE FLOUR

White flour is quick when baking, inexpensive, easily available, and destructive! Almost all bread, pastas, fast food, and baked goods are made with white flour. "While wheat is touted as part of a 'heart healthy diet,' and we are encouraged to eat more whole grains, the wheat we buy in the supermarket is worlds away, genetically speaking, from the wheat our grandparents ate. Not coincidentally, their generation was far leaner and healthier than ours. Clearly, something radical has changed in our national diet and the genetic modification of wheat" according to Dr. William Davis, M.D.

White flour has little or no nutrition and is toxic and an anti-nutrient, much like sugar. The average American eats more than 220 pounds of white flour yearly! Just add the 160 pounds of sugar with 220 pounds of flour, and you have a dietary disaster. Instead of "enriched" flour which was created by our government in 1941, we have "impoverished" flour!

3. PROCESSED FATS AND OILS

Another American mis-conception is that to be healthy we must eat a low-cholesterol, low-fat, or non-fat diet. Rather we need fats and oils, but they must be the right kinds of fats and oils.

When processed oils are heated above 392 degrees, the molecules change shape turning it into a toxic category of fats called trans-fats. And this product is found in almost all supermarket oils. Just think of all the processed foods made with these kinds of oils. It's goodbye to salad dressings, breakfast cereals, crackers, chocolates, candy, potato chips, cookies, donuts, peanut butter, non-dairy creamers, and French fries!

What's a person to do? Don't give up, just yet. There are excellent alternate choices. We all will survive, but it involves making the right food choices.

4. MILK PRODUCTS AND MEATS

Milk's reputation as being a necessary nutrient is probably undeserved. Dr. Frank Oski, former director of the Department of Pediatrics at John's Hopkins University School of Medicine said: "We should all stop drinking milk. It was designed for calves not for humans."

Dr. Russell Bunai, pediatrician, in an issue of National Health said: "The one single change to the United States diet that could provide the greatest health benefits is the elimination of milk products." About 70% of the world's population do not drink milk or consume dairy products like Americans do. Mother's milk is a perfect food for infants, not adults. In nature, no animal drinks milk after weaning, nor does any species drink the milk of another species.

Pasteurization is a prime factor in milk's bad effects because it destroys nutrients and creates toxins. In one study, calves who were fed whole milk remained healthy, but calves fed pasteurized milk typically died within eight weeks.

As you can see, there's a whole lot of bad news when taking a good long hard look at the diets we have fed ourselves and our families. Your good health is priceless. I hope and wish that all of you will live to the ripe old age of 120, just like Moses and Abraham and Isaac and Jacob and a whole host of people in the past. But for all of us today, the promise of God still is good:

> *For all of us (man) are mortal, our (his) days will be a hundred and twenty years!* (Genesis 6:3)

The book *Anatomy of an Illness* was written by Norman Cousins in 1964. Cousins was a layman with no medical or scientific training. He was diagnosed with *ankylosing spondylitis*, a connective tissue disease that deteriorates collagen, the glue that holds our cells together. This disease was literally causing his body to fall apart. His illness was diagnosed by his doctors to be incurable and fatal. He was unwilling to accept this diagnosis, however, so he sought out any knowledge that might help him to treat himself and recover. He succeeded and succeeded so well that he wrote this best selling book about it. In it, Cousins described the actions he took in four areas:

First: He recognized that he was being harmed by his medical treatment and the medications he was prescribed. He concluded that the drugs were so toxic and poisonous that they were accelerating his health decline.

Second: He discovered the enormous power of the mind over the body. The pain he was experiencing was affected by his attitude toward the pain. By learning how to change his attitude, he reduced his pain.

Third: He found that laughter was a powerful therapy. He found that ten minutes of genuine hearty laughter would cause his pain to go away for two or more hours. He watched funny movies, read funny books, watched funny TV, and when the painless effect wore off, he would do it all over again. The laughter and humor had beneficial effects on his body chemistry and contributed to his recovery!

Fourth: He also discovered the powerful anti-inflammatory properties of Vitamin C and took 25 grams per day administered by intravenous drip.

And he made a complete recovery! He believed in the following verse, "A cheerful heart is a good medicine!" (Proverbs 17:22)

Passing the Baton

TAKE AWAY TRUTH: Your good health or bad health has everything to do with your life, your legacy, and your future! You can arm yourself with the latest in research and practice so that you can live in health to really enjoy everything about your four generation legacy! Yes, you can! Yes, there is hope! Yes, there is help for you!

For more information about the issues in this chapter, see Appendix D at the back of this book.

TWELVE

Questions To Ask Yourself

Jesus replied, "I tell you the truth, if you have faith as small as a mustard seed, you can say to this mountain, 'move from here to there' and it will move! Nothing will be impossible for you!" (Matthew 17:20)

The first question is: Do you really believe this promise? Be honest with yourself, do you? This is a huge concept to truly believe. The late Rev. Charles Swindoll, pastor, radio speaker, and writer tells this story:

> In 1959, it was hot! Cynthia and I agreed, we desperately needed an air conditioner in our little apartment. I said, "Let's do this...not tell anybody about our need. Let's just pray."
> Winter passed, spring came...still praying. We went home to visit her folks for a quick two day visit. Nobody knew we were visiting except her folks. Out of the clear blue, a phone call came from a guy who lived across town who had known us before we went to the seminary.
> He said, "Chuck, we've got an almost new air conditioner. Could you use it?"

I thought, "Walk around a wall six times and then on the seventh time, seven times. Is it really possible? Wow...that's the way God operates! He does the impossible!" The little air conditioner lasted four years, the whole time we were in Dallas going to seminary! I wondered, "How did this friend know we were visiting Cynthia's folks?"

Now the really big question: "Why would you 'waste' your life doing something good for God?" You can find lots of stories about people, churches, and institutions doing good things for God...without God! Read any public relations business brochure, pick up a magazine from the lions clubs or rotary clubs, and you will see that without God, they have done good things for and in this world! Sad to say, you can also find stories about good churches and good religious organizations who are doing good things for God too but without God's help! Many churches in America could be run well by a secular business manager with good moral values. Why? Because they are doing quite well without God's help. (Oh, yes, they will all deny the above indictment.)

What about you and your family and your future—can you get along without God's help? We can go about life, pay our tithes, do our devotions, tuck our kids into bed with a prayer, attend church, live a good moral life, have a good marriage, enjoy good character, be generous, and help out elderly neighbors—all without God's help.

Back to "the" question: Why would you waste your life

doing good things for God when you could be doing the impossible with God's help? I'm willing to put money on the line that you didn't think about this question this morning or maybe this question has never crossed your mind.

Dr. David Gibbs, lawyer and founder of the Christian Legal Association (CLA), an organization that without remuneration defends Christians who may be caught in a lawsuit because of their belief system asked that question. A lawyer—not a preacher—brought me up short and shattered my comfortable Christianity. This kind of question is like velcro in the mind. It sticks for a long, long time.

Perhaps in our journey into four generation legacy building, you thought, "It is impossible; it can't be done because of my situation." This is the moment for another honesty check. With God's help, you can do the impossible!

Let's delve into the world of the impossible by taking a short Bible reading break. Read a story of the impossible becoming possible: Jesus feeds the 5,000 and walks on water—two impossible feats.

God Does the Impossible
(Matt. 14:13-21)

Jesus took a boat ride to escape the crowds, but they followed on foot and were waiting when He landed, "He had compassion on them, and healed their sick." This story begins with the first impossible—healing their sick!

Passing the Baton

The crowd, like all crowds was hungry! It's late and no nearby McDonalds! "Jesus, what are we going to do?" How would you like to have heard His answer? "You give them something to eat."

Okay, Lord, we have searched the crowd and found only one lunch, a little boy who came prepared because his mama packed "only five loaves of bread and two fish." The crowd is said to number 5,000, but there's another problem, in that day, they only counted the men. Where there are 5,000 men, likely you will have 5,000 women; and with 5,000 men and 5,000 women, they will have produced probably 10,000 to 20,000 hungry kids. Let's say conservatively, there's about 20,000 to 30,000 hungry folk. But what is a small lunch among so many? "Loaves" needs a bit of looking into. These loaves were not grocery or bakery loaves, they were more like small buns—five fish-wiches, hardly enough to satisfy one hungry man, let alone his wife and three kids!

Impossible, don't you agree? Jesus said, "Bring them here to Me!" Here's a first clue—where do you take the impossible situations in your life? Jesus blessed the boy's lunch and gave the blessed lunch to twelve astonished men who in turn gave fish-wiches to everybody! "They all ate and were satisfied!" Some of you would have had a half a dozen or more, so how many fish-wiches did they serve that day? One more thing to take note: "And the disciples picked up twelve basketfuls of broken pieces that were left over!" Jesus is concerned that nothing is to be wasted, and I like to think that each of the twelve needed a reminder to take home so that every time they looked at the empty basket hanging on the wall, they remembered the impossible feast!

God can and will do the impossible! This truth does not stand only on this situation: "What is impossible with men and women is possible with God" (Luke 18:27).

Another question comes to mind about right now: How can a man or woman do the impossible? (Read again Matthew 14:22-33.)

Now it's time for the disciples to go home and home is across the sea of Galilee, about three hours by boat on a good day. "Immediately (after they had picked up the pieces), Jesus made the disciples get into the boat and go on ahead of Him to the other side." Then "Jesus went by Himself to pray."

So the disciples set out across the sea of Galilee, and a storm blew up. (Keep in mind that most of these guys were professional sailors, commercial fishermen who earned their living on the Galilee. No beginners here!) Winds were coming at them from all directions, tossing the boat in monster waves! These tough, weathered, macho guys were terrified.

When they saw Jesus walking across the water toward them, they cried out, "It's a ghost!" They were paralyzed with fear!

In these impossible situations, a man, yes, a man who was human just like all of us is about to do the impossible!

Have you ever attempted to take a water walk? (I know, you can walk on water if you live in Minnesota in the winter, but other than that, have you ever attempted to walk on water in liquid form?) It is very important that you don't miss how Peter did the impossible!

Another question: do you currently face something impossible in your life? In your family? In your church? In your business? In your physical body? Watch closely to the four concepts, the four steps when doing the impossible with God's help:

1. YOU MUST ASK!

Ask specifically! Peter didn't say, "If it's okay with You, I might enjoy a walk on the water." He didn't say, "If You are not too busy, just give me a little blessing." He said, "Lord, if it's You, tell me to come to You on the water!"

One day a small business owner gathered his family about the dinner table and announced to them, "I believe the Lord is directing me to do the impossible!" He had their undivided attention. "I am asking the Lord to make it possible for us to live on 10% of our income while we give the Lord 90% of our income!"

Immediately there was a strong reaction, "Do the math...we can't live on 10%...it is impossible...we just can't do it!" He had just begun a small business in the garage.

Impossible? The next Sunday, he wrote a check to his church for 90% of that week's income! To this day, he still writes the 90% check to his church! But that's not the end of this story. On the 10% they have left over to live on, they currently fully support three hundred full time missionaries! This is not a mistake, three hundred full time missionaries is right. Impossible? Not with God!

Ask with specificity: tell me to come to You, on the water! The Bible says, "You have not because you ask not!" (James 4:2, KJV) No, this is not a blank check for you to squander it on yourself. No, it's not that you selfishly want to be billionaire! "When you ask, you do not receive, because you ask with wrong motives, that you may spend what you get on your pleasures" (James 4:3).

Ask specifically...but ask with the right motives! This is not a selfish presumption; it is not a wild wish; it is not a whim; it is not a mere want. Ask with the right motives, and you will receive!

2. DON'T ASK FOR THE STORMY CONDITIONS TO IMPROVE!

"Lord, I'll be so excited and happy to walk on the water to you, but first please make the conditions better so I can walk on the water with you!" This is not stated, but I believe it to be implied in the story. Isn't it interesting that it was only Peter who asked the Lord to allow him to walk on the water? The storm, likely, scared them all. What were the other disciples thinking at this point?

"Lord, still the storm and then I'll come to you!" Even if the conditions of life were absolutely perfect, you still can't walk on water! Maybe you, like me, have spent too much of your lifetime asking God to improve the conditions. "God, when the bills are paid, then I will tithe… when things are smooth, I'll witness about You to my neighbor…when my family situations are just right, then we will begin a family altar…when I can find just the right kind of a church, then You'll see me and my family there on a regular basis…when my health is better, I might be able to take that overseas missions trip…when I find the right spouse, then together we will live for You, Lord…and on and on it goes.

I've spent my life asking for the "just right" conditions, but they are never just right! God always does the impossible when the conditions are not good! Your conditions will never be without bumps on the sea of life! No, not ever! Forget about the conditions, God still can do the impossible in spite of circumstances, even in the perfect storm!

3. YOU MUST LET GO OF YOUR PLAN B (or C or D or even Z)!

"Peter, this is not a good night to walk on water!" It's dark…it's wet…it's cold…it's a storm like we've never experienced…conditions are impossible…you're scared to death so don't leave the boat!

If I had been there, I would have asked, "Lord, I might walk on water, but please come closer, come right over here!" Why? Just in case it doesn't work, I could always grab the boat. What about you? "Lord, I'll come, but first let me get my life jacket on!"

I always want Plan B or any other plan in place before

I attempt to walk on water. Church boards are great at saying, "Preacher, the conditions aren't good, what is your plan B?" Lawyers always advise against water walking unless you have your back-up plan. Counselors will help guide you in formulating your next plan. Teachers and or professors are great with cautionary advice. And then of course, parents will ask for your Plan B.

Why be ordinary when you could walk on water? "Peter, do you have your Plan B in mind?" No...I just have Jesus! That's all! That's enough! What more do I need? Jesus is all I need!

> *But when you ask, you must believe and not doubt, because the one who doubts is like a wave of the sea, blown and tossed by the wind* (James 1:6).

Why have a Plan B when you have Jesus?

4. YOU MUST GET OUT OF THE BOAT!

You don't get out of the boat until you have heard the divine "Come, He said!" We are not talking about foolishness or presumption. When you have the okay from the Lord Himself, it's time to get out of the boat! It's time to break free from your box!

The biggest obstacle we face in doing the impossible is fear! What if God lets me drown? What if it doesn't work? What will my friends say? What if I miserably fail and fall flat? Fear takes all kinds to forms. There's the fear of the unknown! What does the Bible have to say about fear? "Perfect love (His love) casts out fear because fear has torment" (I John 4:18). "You will not fear the terror of night" (Psalm 91:5).

You do not have to be afraid of the storm just because the boat is rocking, pitching from side to side, bucking up and down with the wind swirling, wet cold spray drenching you, darkness you can feel. You can do the impossible with God's help. You can step out of the boat! You can leave your comfort zone!

Then Peter got down out of the boat, walked on the water and came toward Jesus! Peter, a man just as human as we are, a man who miserably failed, walked on the water! Two people in all of the world's history, walked on the water—Jesus and Peter with the Lord's help! Awesome!

However, you might have spotted the problem and maybe have focused on the problem: "But when Peter saw the wind, he was afraid and beginning to sink...Lord, save me!" We can't see the wind, but it's so easy to see the actions of wind. It's too easy to spot the problems in our needs that makes the situation an impossibility. And the devil, along with your family, friends, and neighbors, will be quick to point to the storm and the impossibilities you might currently be facing. It's not easy to get out of the boat!

But Jesus is wonderful! "Jesus reached out His hand and caught him!" Never lose sight of the fact that the two men walked on the water back to the boat. There was no rebuke for Peter's doubt, only help to finish the walk on

Questions To Ask Yourself

the water! "And when they climbed into the boat, the wind died down!"

Don't overlook this: He asked Peter, "Why did you doubt?" That's a question for all of us. Why doubt when you have His word? Why doubt that He is able to do the impossible?

Pastor David, the senior pastor of a large church in the south, tells this story: It was a Wednesday night service and at the end he made an altar call and among those who came forward was Marcie. She had just graduated from Bible college and is home and attends church that night with her parents. She motions for the pastor to come down to speak with her. She says, "Pastor, I have surrendered my life to go to the mission field."

He says, "Marcie, that is so wonderful. Where are you going?"

She says, "To Malaysia, to a tribe of head-hunters, people eaters because they have not had a missionary in the past eleven years." He replies, "Marcie…you?" He thinks, "Here is this beautiful, petite, tiny, frail girl, and she is going to be eaten! I'm not ever going…they eat people and if I go I could feed the entire village for a week or more!" (Pastor David is a former Green Beret, a decorated veteran.) "I'm not going, but she is!"

She says, "Pastor, please lay your hands on me and bless me."

At this time, her parents rush up to the pastor and

plead, "Please talk some sense to her. Talk her out of this. This is impossible!"

She replies, with tears streaming down her face, "I know. But I am going. God has called me." With that she drops to her knees and bows her head. He calls for the elders to join him and together they pray for Marcie.

He thinks, as he prays, "Oh, God, this is an impossible situation. If she goes, Lord, spare her, don't let her suffer if they capture her for their sacrifice. If I have given anybody a death sentence, Lord this is it."

Marcie had done some language study in preparation, but she needed someone to go with her. She asked the pastor to help find her a helper or even a couple. When they hear about where she is planning to go, all refuse except a set of grandparents who will go with her as far as the helicopter ride but not any farther.

Thirty days go by and no mission board is willing to send her on this suicide mission. She makes her plans, raises the money needed, and sets the dates. You need to understand that the only way in is by helicopter, but there's a problem. The chopper can't land because these natives have discovered that with their spears they can disable the blades and cause it to crash and then they eat the crew. The last missionary was eaten by this tribe eleven years previously. Oil and mineral explorations in this area have even been halted because of the danger.

The plan is to take the chopper in and hover at 150 to 200 feet off the ground and let Marcie rappel down to the mountain top, something she had never done.

The chopper arrives at the clearing, and the co-pilot is holding the chopper level with the "collector" stick. They throw out two duffel bags with her equipment and clothes. Now it's time for Marcie to rappel down. This seasoned pilot, who by his own admission, has never cried over anything, begins to bawl. He says to the grandparents, "Tell her goodbye; you'll never see her again." Then they snap her to the 150 feet of rope and down she goes. The pilot told her, "I'll be back in sixty days, at the same place, but you won't be here. Please think again, don't go!" But down she goes despite the warning.

Sixty days later the chopper flies in and hovers over the clearing, and there is Marcie standing and waving along with more than seventy head-hunter converts!

The rest of the story? Nobody knew that these head-hunters only ate men! When she hit the ground, they fell to their knees and began to worship her! They had a 200-year-old legend that told them that one day a female god would drop from the sky with a special word for them!

Marcie told them, "I am not a god, but I come from God and have a message for you from Him!" She said that it was the easiest soul-winning she had ever done!

But what really gets me in this true story is that as she was about to leave the chopper, the seasoned, veteran pilot pleads again with her, "Marcie, don't go because you will never come back!"

She replied, "You don't understand. I have been called by God to go! I was not called to come back!

Passing the Baton

Why do you want to waste your life by merely doing something good for God when you could do the impossible with God's help?

For the eyes of the Lord range throughout the earth to strengthen those whose hearts are fully committed to Him! (II Chronicles 16:9)

Jesus looked at them and said, "With man this is impossible, but with God all things are possible!" (Matthew 19:26)

**WITH GOD'S HELP,
YOU CAN AND YOU WILL
BUILD A FOUR GENERATION
LEGACY!**

APPENDIX A

Suggested Blessings To Use

FOUNDATIONAL BLESSINGS

> The Lord bless you and keep you; the Lord make His face shine upon you and be gracious to you; the Lord turn His face toward you and give you peace!

This blessing, as transliterated from the Hebrew into English, means:

> THE LORD BLESS YOU AND KEEP YOU
> (Yahweh, make your property increase and guard you from all the evil going on around you.)

> THE LORD MAKE HIS FACE SHINE UPON YOU, AND BE GRACIOUS TO YOU;
> (Yahweh, grant wisdom and kindness to you and your children's children.)

> THE LORD TURN HIS FACE TOWARD YOU AND GIVE YOU PEACE!
> (Yahweh, suppress divine anger and bestow favor upon you and give you shalom!)

Shalom means: Completeness, wholeness, health,

peace, welfare, safety, soundness, tranquility, prosperity, perfectness, fullness, rest, harmony and contentment.

I will make you into a great nation and I will bless you;
I will make your name great, and you will be a blessing;
I will bless those who bless you, and whoever curses you I will curse;
And all peoples on earth will be blessed through you!

When you worship and bless the Lord:
Praise the LORD, O my soul,
    and forget not all His benefits...
Who forgives all my sins and heals all my diseases,
Who redeems my life from the pit and crowns me
    with love and compassion,
Who satisfies my desires with good things
So that my youth is renewed like the eagle's!

But from everlasting to everlasting
The Lord's love is with me when I fear You,
For Your righteousness with my children's children...
With all of them who keep Your covenants
    and remember to obey Your precepts!

THE JEWISH BLESSINGS FOR BOYS AND GIRLS
May God make you as Ephraim and Manassah.
May God make you as Sarah, Leah, Rebekah and Rachel.

SOME SAMPLE BLESSINGS
I bless you with laughter, so you may fill the world with it.
I bless you with joy, so you can give it to others.
I bless you with good communication skills,
    so you can shine light into other lives.
I bless you with compassion.
I bless you with wisdom.
I bless you with understanding.
I bless you with the favor of others
    and most of all, the favor of God.
I bless you with love.

In the name of Jesus, I bless you...
With a new beginning!
With new thinking!
With a new purpose in life!
With the blessing of God
    so that you can and will pass the blessing to others.

I bless you with a godly future.
I bless you with the favor of God
    as well as favor with people you touch in life.
I bless you with divine protection at all times.
I bless you with joy of heaven.
I bless you with a long and fruitful life.
I bless you with my love and devotion
    as well as the love of the Lord.
I bless you with divine mercy and goodness

to follow you all the days of your long life
so that together we may someday dwell
in the house of the Lord, forever!

Of all the blessings I can give you...
I pray you will know Jesus Christ and have eternal life!
Of all the blessings I can give you...
I pray you will be blameless in character
    and live a productive life!
Of all the blessings I can give you...
I pray you will have a mind to work, a spirit of excellence
    in all you do, to walk in God's will with your life
    and a spirit of joy and happiness in your life work!
I have blessed you in the all powerful name of Jesus Christ,
    who, through His life and death has made it possible
    for you to experience all of these blessings!

Some ways in which you can bless your children by inserting his or her name where there is a blank. You can do this with blessings based on scriptures:

Blessed _____ will be because
    you do not walk in the counsel of the wicked,
    nor do you stand in the path of sinners,
    nor do you sit in the seat of scoffers.
But as your parents, we have seen you delight
    in the law of the Lord.
You have been thinking about His law often.

May God bless you, _____,
   like a tree planted by the streams of water.
May God allow you to grow and bear His fruit in His
   season and that your life will not wither and whatever
   you will do, it will prosper!
   (This blessing is based on Psalm 1)

I bless you _____ with a special effort
   that will add to your faith, goodness;
   and to goodness, knowledge and wisdom;
   and to knowledge, self-control; and to self control,
      perseverance;
   and to your perseverance, godliness;
   and to your godliness, brotherly (sisterly)
      kindness to all others;
   and to your kindness, love, mercy, and grace.
When you, _____, possess these qualities
   that are growing in your life, they will keep you from
   being ineffective and unproductive in your life and
   in your knowledge of your Lord, Jesus Christ!
   (This blessing is based on II Peter 1:5-9)

I bless you_____ with the joy of the Lord.
I bless you with gentleness to all others.
I bless you with a thankful heart at all times.
I bless you with the peace of God that will
   guard your heart and mind.
I bless you _____ with what is true, what is noble,

what is right, what is pure, what is admirable, what is
 excellent so that you can and will think about such
 things.
I bless your thought life to think about such things.
And whatever you have learned from (me or us)
 or seen in me that is good, put it into practice
 and the God of all peace will be with you
 now and forever!
(This blessing is based on Philippians 4)

This is a powerful way to bless—use your creativity.

APPENDIX B

BUILDING YOUR PLAN for a four generation legacy. Please list on a separate page your answers to the following questions:

The VISION statement:
How we plan to build our four-generation legacy:

The first generation, my spouse and I, what we must do to begin laying the first generational foundation:

The second generation...our children. What and how we will pass our life concepts to them so they can pass on the legacy:

The third generation...our grandchildren. What we plan to do to help our children build the legacy concepts in this generation. What we do in a positive way to supplement and strengthen legacy building:

The fourth generation...our great-grandchildren. Plans to insure that the legacy is understood and passed on to the following generation. What will be our role in the life of this fourth generation. How we can help the original vision to be renewed:

APPENDIX C

We raise our children, grandchildren, and great-grandchildren in truth and righteousness so that the blessing can be transferred forward. It is so that a heritage, a legacy, and a dynasty can be passed on. Fill in the specifics of the following for your family on a separate page:

OUR HERITAGE:

OUR LEGACY:

OUR DYNASTY:

APPENDIX D

Atkins, Robert C., M.D., DR. ATKINS' NEW DIET REVOLUTION, M. Evans and Company, Inc., New York, New York, 10017

Colbert, Don, M.D., BIBLE CURE SERIES; Toxic Relief; Reversing Diabetes; I Can Do This Diet; and The Seven Pillars of Health. Strang Publications, Winter Park, Florida

Campbell, Colin T., THE CHINA STUDY: The Most Comprehensive Study of Nutrition Ever Conducted And the Startling Implications for Diet

Davis, Kara, M.D., SPIRITUAL SECRETS to a Healthy Heart, Siloam, Strang Publications, Winter Park, Florida, online and in E-Book format

Davis, William, M.D., WHEAT BELLY: Lose the Wheat, Lose the Weight and Find Your Path Back to Health

Francis, Raymond M.Sc., NEVER BE SICK AGAIN, One Disease, Two Causes, Six Pathways, Health Communications, Inc., Deerfield Beach, FL

Francis, Raymond, M.Sc. And King, Michelle King, NEVER BE FAT AGAIN, The 6-WEEK Cellular SOLUTION to Permanently Break the Fat Cycle, Health Communications, Inc. Deerfield Beach , FL

Francis, Raymond, M.Sc., NEVER FEAR CANCER AGAIN, How to Prevent and Reverse Cancer, Health Communications, Inc., Deerfield Beach, FL

Hoffman, Jay, HUNZA: Secrets of the World's Healthiest and Oldest Living People, Clinton, NJ: New Win Publishing

Mayo Clinic, THE MAYO CLINIC DIET: Eat Well, Enjoy Life, Lose Weight by Mayo Clinic, Rochester, MN

Strand, Robert, THE B WORD, The Purpose and Power of the Blessing, Evergreen Press, Mobile, Alabama, 800-367-8203

Strand, Robert, BREAKING GENERATIONAL CURSES, How to Receive Healing for Yourself and Your Family, Evergreen Press, Mobile, Alabama, 800-367-8203 (Book Two in The Power of the Blessing series)

Any of the above resources should get you moving in the right direction as you begin or continue your life's journey to the 120 year mark! If your local bookstores doesn't have it, they can order any one or more of these for you. Better yet, go on Google.com or Amazon.com or most all of these authors have books available on an internet site.

About the Author

ROBERT STRAND is the author of more than 60 books, and his "Moments To Give" series has sold more than a million copies. A consummate storyteller, Robert knows how to blend the emotional impact of true stories with practical insights from his many years of pastoral experience to produce breakthrough results. He and his wife, Donna, live in Springfield, Missouri.

Other books by Robert Strand from Evergreen Press

The B Word
Breaking Generational Curses
Desperate Housewives of the Bible—Old Testament
Desperate Housewives of the Bible—New Testament
Angel at My Door
In the Company of Angels
Angels Unaware
The Power of Forgiving
The Power of Motherhood
The Power of Fatherhood
The Power of Grandparenting
The Power of Gift Giving
The Power of Thanksgiving
The Power of Debt Free Living
Pearl Dust
Live Fully, Laugh Often…and Don't Forget To Let the Cats Out!